From *Ancient* Text
to *Valid* Application

From *Ancient* Text
to *Valid* Application

A Practical Exploration of Pericopal Theology in Preaching

JOSIAH D. BOYD

Foreword by Abraham Kuruvilla

WIPF & STOCK · Eugene, Oregon

FROM *ANCIENT* TEXT TO *VALID* APPLICATION
A Practical Exploration of Pericopal Theology in Preaching

Wipf & Stock
An Imprint of Wipf and Stock Publishers
199 W. 8th Ave., Suite 3
Eugene, OR 97401

www.wipfandstock.com

PAPERBACK ISBN: 978-1-6667-2514-8
HARDCOVER ISBN: 978-1-6667-2041-9
EBOOK ISBN: 978-1-6667-2042-6

11/03/21

To all who,
filled with the *Spirit* of God,
stand before the *people* of God,
open the *word* of God
to herald the gospel of the *Son* of God
for the *glory* of God.

Contents

Foreword

DECLARED ARISTOTLE IN THE fourth century BCE: "There are necessarily three kinds of rhetorical speeches, deliberative, forensic, and epideictic" (*Rhetoric* 1.3). From the days of this sage onward, all public speech was thus conceived as the rhetoric of legislatures (deliberative), the rhetoric of courts (forensic), or the rhetoric reserved for formal occasions of festivity or grief that praised the value of a celebrated or mourned individual (epideictic).

It was with the Hebrews, early in their history, followed later by Christians, that a new form of public address arose: the exposition of a sacred text. In their respective communities, the synagogue and the church, this kind of speech achieved prominence and developed into a new genre of communication. The difference between the forms of classical rhetoric and that of sacred rhetoric, for our purposes, was precisely this: the former, categorized in the Aristotelian triplet was purely topical, while the latter was not, constrained as it was by a particular text. Thus, preaching of Scripture stood apart, simply because of the critical importance to the community of a text construed as the word of God. Only in this category was the exposition of a text foundational to the address employed, coupled with exhortations to listeners to respond to those sacred texts. And thus a new form of rhetoric was birthed!

In this science and art, where exposition of a sacred text and exhortation to action are central, the crucial task of the expositor and exhorter is to discover valid application for a modern audience from an ancient text. Unfortunately, throughout most of the two millennia of the church age, this has been the missing link in every theory of Bible interpretation. A hermeneutic for making this move from ancient text to modern audience with exegetical rigor has been lacking. So the lot of the homiletician is not easy: each week, this brave soul has to negotiate the formidable passage from the *then* of the text to the *now* of the audience—a burdensome responsibility.

However, in the last five decades, the understanding of how language works has grown exponentially. The light has begun to shine! Communication of any kind—sacred or secular, spoken or scripted—is increasingly being recognized as a communicator *doing* something with what is communicated. Thus, even in Scripture, its authors *do* things with their words. In other words, there is a distinction between *sentence meaning* (i.e., semantics: grammar, vocabulary, and syntax) and *utterance meaning* (i.e., pragmatics: what the author/speaker is *doing* with what he is saying). These inferential operations of pragmatics are integral to interpretation *for application*, which is every preacher's onus. Only after discerning the pragmatics of a text, i.e., the *doings* of the author(s), can one proceed to valid application.

Because authorial *doings* (pragmatics) in Scripture speak of God and how he relates to his creation, I called these authorial *doings* in/with texts *theology*, the theology of the particular pericope chosen as the preaching text *pericopal theology*. To live by pericopal theology is to accept God's gracious invitation to be aligned to the will of God as depicted in each pericope.

So, each sermon must point out the theology of the pericope under consideration, elucidating what that specific text affirms about God and his relationship with mankind. Biblical interpretation for application that does not elucidate this crucial intermediary, pericopal theology, is *de facto* incomplete, for without discerning this entity by pragmatic inference from the text, valid application can never be arrived at.

Only one person, the Lord Jesus Christ, perfectly met every aspect of God's will, being without sin. That is to say Jesus Christ alone has comprehensively abided by the theology of every pericope of Scripture. One may then say that each pericope of the Bible is actually portraying a characteristic of Christ (a pixel of Christ's image), showing us what it means to perfectly fulfill, as he did, the particular call of that pericope. The Bible as a whole, the collection of all its pericopes, then, portrays what a perfect human looks like, exemplified by Jesus Christ, God incarnate, the perfect man. The written word of God, in this manner, depicts the incarnate Word of God.

Thus, pericope by pericope and sermon by sermon, as God's people are aligned to the image of Christ displayed in each pericope, they become progressively more Christlike. Preaching, therefore, facilitates the conformation of the children of God into the image of the Son of God by the power of God. After all, that is God's ultimate goal for his children, to be "conformed to the image [*eikōn*] of his Son" in his humanity (Rom 8:29). That, I submit, is the primary function of God's word and, therefore, the primary purpose of preaching. I have, therefore, labeled this hermeneutic for preaching *christiconic*.

And with such a christiconic interpretation of Scripture preaching also becomes Trinitarian in concept and function. The text inspired by God the Holy Spirit depicts God the Son, to whose image mankind is to conform.

In so being conformed, the will of God the Father is being done and his kingdom coming to pass.

Thus, preaching is not merely for the information of minds, but for the transformation of lives—that they may be conformed to the image of Christ, in the power of the Holy Spirit, through the instrumentality of Scripture, by the agency of the preacher. Sermon by sermon, habits are changed, dispositions are created, character is built, the image of Christ is formed, and humans are becoming what they were meant by God to be.

Over the years, the notions of pericopal theology and christiconic hermeneutic have come to be backed by a substantial hermeneutic. However, the issue of its practical testing was still to be undertaken. Linus Torvalds, the creator and main developer of Linux, once said: "Theory and practice sometimes clash. And when that happens, theory loses. Every single time." I'm glad to report, via *From Ancient Text to Valid Application*, that theory and practice together have won this round! The issue of the degree of success potentially achievable by such a hermeneutic in an actual preaching situation has now been settled.

"Can the implementation of pericopal theology and a christiconic hermeneutic aid in a preacher's identification and communication of valid application and the hearer's comprehension of that application?" The answer to Josiah Boyd's research question is an emphatic "Yes!" His surveyed audience of churchgoers demonstrated a statistically significant increase in comprehension not just of biblical knowledge (53 percent increase) but, pertinent to the topic at hand, also of their understanding of pericopal theology (182.5 percent increase) and its applicational implications (412 percent increase)! Remarkable, indeed! Measurable growth certainly occurred as a result of preaching with a pericopal theology and christiconic hermeneutic.

Boyd's is the first attempt to delineate the effectiveness of preaching a particular narrative text, the book of Jonah, by employing the notions of pericopal theology and a christiconic hermeneutic in a specific church situation. The results demonstrated herein resoundingly affirm the manifest value of preaching in this fashion. Such an outcome serves as strong encouragement to preachers to engage pericopal theology in their weekly sermonic undertakings. If the theory itself is not an adequate motivator, surely Boyd's study of the practice in *From Ancient Text to Valid Application* will convince expositors to move in this fruitful direction—a direction that, I am convinced, edifies God's people, extends the kingdom of God's Son, and exalts God, redounding to his glory. May it ever be so!

ABRAHAM KURUVILLA

Professor of Christian Preaching

The Southern Baptist Theological Seminary, Louisville, Kentucky

Acknowledgments

THANK YOU, GOD'S PEOPLE at Church of the Open Bible in Swift Current, Saskatchewan, and at Oakridge Bible Chapel in Oakville, Ontario, for providing the motivation, encouragement, patience, and support that aided the completion of this work.

Thank you, Dr. Abraham Kuruvilla, for asking good questions, seeking godly answers, writing challenging prose, modeling faithful preaching, and encouraging many others (myself included) to do likewise.

Thank you, Patricia, my wife, and my family, for being my chief partners in ministry.

Thank you, my Lord, for being "a gracious and compassionate God, slow to anger and abundant in lovingkindness" (Jonah 4:2).

1

Introduction to the Issue

THE IMPORTANCE OF THE WORD PREACHED

IT IS DIFFICULT TO overstate the necessity of the centrality of the word of God preached—and preached *well*—in the life of any local expression of the body of Christ. As a child needs nutrient-rich calories to grow in a healthy way, so God's people experience maturation through consistent, Spirit-empowered feedings from the Bible prepared by a capable, Spirit-filled chef (Matt 4:4; Acts 2:42; 1 Cor 2:1–5; 3:1–2; Heb 5:11–14; 1 Pet 2:2–3).[1] It was for this reason Paul emphatically charged Timothy, an overseer of a local congregation, with the task of unwaveringly and unrelentingly "preach[ing] the word" (2 Tim 4:1–2),[2] the wholly inspired and wholly useful self-revelation of a holy

1. While an articulation of the importance of expository preaching in the life of the church has been offered by many, for a few accessible samples, see Dever, *Nine Marks of a Healthy Church*, 39–55; Jorgenson, "Necessity of Contemporary Preaching"; and Allen, "Expository Preaching." Obviously, not all written works with the label "preaching" attached offer the kind of preaching that is necessary for the life of the church. Not all preaching is created equal (more on this in chapter 2). One of the aims of the work you now hold in your hands is to explore and articulate one hermeneutic and homiletic that lends itself to the kind of preaching that *is* essential and, therefore, *must* be central in the life of any given local expression of the body of Christ.

2. For the purposes of this study, "preaching" refers to the reading, explanation, and application of a portion of God's word in the corporate gathering of God's people for the purpose of changing their lives, by the power of God's Spirit, to conform with the image of God's Son. For a detailed discussion on κηρύσσω specifically and its use in the New Testament regarding proclamation, see Griffiths, *Preaching in the New Testament*, 27–32.

God (3:16), and training others to do likewise (2:2), "accurately handling the word of truth" (2:15). It is by faithfully fulfilling this God-prescribed practice that the people of God are increasingly made "adequate, equipped for every good work" (3:17).

This same apostolic exhortation, carried upon the breath of the Holy Spirit, from whom it originally came (2 Pet 1:20–21), has reverberated through two millennia of church history and even now lands with a weighty thud in the laps of those today who dare to don a pulpit with the intention of shepherding the people of God: "Preach the word!" Notice that both the conduit of delivery (i.e., preaching) and the content of the message (i.e., the word) have been divinely established within that three-word charge.[3] Just as when a doctor says, "Take two pills orally with food," she has marked the path that leads toward better health by providing both the specific medicine and the specific means of its ingestion, so too God when he prescribes the preaching of the word. Thus, "[n]o preacher, regardless of where he serves, is free to reinvent preaching."[4] To do so would be tantamount to ignoring the doctor and, instead, trying to take the antibiotic through means of absorption rather than ingestion. Not only will it not work, but it makes the patient look foolish for thinking it might. No, a wise patient follows the doctor's instructions if health is the goal. Similarly, if spiritual health is the goal, God's people best obey the Doctor. One can rightly conclude that God's word is of such importance for the health of God's people that God himself made sure to communicate the ideal method of its administration.

Perhaps another illustration will serve to communicate the importance of the issue at hand. Imagine if parents, ignoring all the advice and guidelines of dieticians and nutritionists, decide to raise their children on Tang and gummy bears. No doubt the children will voice their approval, and there may be a period of time in which the negative effects of such eating habits are largely unseen. But, make no mistake, there will be a price to pay. Teeth will fall out. Body fat will increase. Energy levels will suffer. Cognitive functioning will be impeded. In short, the children will fail to develop as they should because someone, who should have known better, ignored the simple, straightforward advice of the experts around them.

---

3. While preaching will take different forms in different pulpits in different parts of the world in different eras, it remains *preaching* (i.e., the declaration of God's truth to God's people). As Adams warns, "Whenever preachers depart from the purpose and the intent of a biblical portion, to that extent they lose their authority to preach. In short, the purpose of reading, explaining, and applying a portion of Scripture is to obey the command to 'preach the Word.'" *Preaching with Purpose*, 19.

4. Lawson, *Kind of Preaching God Blesses*, 31.

So it is in the household of God. Pastors are to feed God's children following the recommendations and guidelines the Expert has provided. God knows best how his children must be fed and what must be on the menu in order to best facilitate healthy growth and steady maturation. To add, subtract, or alter either the authorized or the inspired message is to do so at the expense of those who need the nutrients (i.e., the members of the family of God). Sure, there may be a period of time in which the negative effects are largely unseen, and the immature may even voice their appreciation for the junk food diet (2 Tim 4:3). But, ultimately, they will suffer from malnourishment, leading to stunted development (Heb 5:12–14), increased vulnerabilities (2 Pet 2:1; 1 John 4:1), and dangerous maladies (1 Cor 11:30) that could have otherwise been avoided had the word been preached—and preached *well*.

Well-fed sheep grow as they ought; misfed sheep do not. To express this reality another way, "The spiritual life of any congregation . . . will never exceed the high-water mark set by its pulpit."[5] As the physical health of a child will struggle to exceed the contents of the meals he is served, so too the spiritual health of the people of a church will struggle to exceed the contents of the preaching under which they sit. It is via the consistent and public model provided for them by their God-appointed shepherds that the people of God learn to hear from God, understand God, obey God, and be conformed to the image of the Son of God. It is the goings-on in the pulpit, and the handling, treatment, and use of the word of God therein, that both showcases and dictates the values of any given local body of believers.

In sum, biblical preaching is crucial for the edification of the individual Christian and for the body of Christ as a whole (Eph 4:11–16). However, aside from the content of the sermon being shaped by the word of God, what does biblical preaching look like? What must preaching include if it is to be labeled "faithful"? Certainly, preaching the word assumes the reading of the word and the explanation of the word, but does faithful preaching also include the application of the word? Is the job of the preacher fully complete if the text is left unapplied? It is to these latter questions that this study now turns.

---

5. Lawson, *Kind of Preaching God Blesses*, 16. Other forms of "word intake" (e.g., small group Bible study, personal devotions, sermon podcasts, etc.), as beneficial as they may be for the Christian, do nothing to diminish the necessity of preaching. This is because the latter has the *telos* of the application of a particular text to a particular group of people by a particular shepherd who has been given by God to said people. As Griffiths writes, "Preaching is necessary and vital—but not all-sufficient—for the nourishment and edification of the local church." *Preaching in the New Testament*, 133.

THE IMPORTANCE OF THE WORD APPLIED

> But prove yourselves doers of the word, and not merely hearers
> who delude themselves. For if anyone is a hearer of the word
> and not a doer, he is like a man who looks at his natural face in a
> mirror; for once he has looked at himself and gone away, he has
> immediately forgotten what kind of person he was. But one who
> looks intently at the perfect law, the law of liberty, and abides by
> it, not having become a forgetful hearer but an effectual doer,
> this man will be blessed in what he does. (Jas 1:22–25)

With these words the apostle James warns followers of Jesus Christ that
what God commands in his word must change the way they live their lives.[6]
"If the Word implanted is dynamic, working salvation, it is imperative that
believers do what the Word says."[7] The very nature of the word demands
application as through the diligent, Spirit-empowered application of God's
word the person of God is "progressively and increasingly aligned with the
will of God, becoming conformed to the image of the Son of God."[8] To use
the language that James himself employs, God's people are to look "intently"
at God's word and "abide by it." God has revealed his will to his people in his
word and, as such, expects intentional, gradual, and continual conformity to
it by way of intentional consideration of it.

The result of such intentional and compliant application of God's word
is, according to James, blessedness, not only in the future but in the present
(see also Matt 5:3–11; John 13:17). "Those who are blessed by God live in
the union of truth and action, which is their joy."[9] It is a blessing to creatures
to live obediently before their Creator. Psalm 1 describes the relationship
between obedience and blessing, once again centered around God's word:

> How blessed is the man who does not walk in the counsel of the
> wicked,
> Nor stand in the path of sinners,
> Nor sit in the seat of scoffers!

---

6. That James is writing to regenerate Christians is clear: "To the twelve tribes" (1:1),
"brethren" (1:2, 16, 19; 2:1, 14; 3:1, 10, 12; 4:11; 5:7, 9, 10, 12, 19), "brother" (1:9; 2:15;
4:11[x2]), "beloved" (2:5). In addition to how the apostle refers to his audience, there
are also a number of imperatives he places upon them that would not likely be extended
to unbelievers (e.g., "consider it all joy" [1:2], "let endurance have its perfect result"
[1:4], "But if any of you lacks wisdom, let him ask of God" [1:5], "do not hold your faith
in our glorious Lord Jesus Christ with an attitude of personal favoritism" [2:1]).

7. Richardson, *James*, 94.

8. Kuruvilla, *Manual for Preaching*, 59.

9. Richardson, *James*, 98.

But his delight is in the law of the LORD,
And in His law he meditates day and night.
He will be like a tree firmly planted by streams of water,
Which yields its fruit in its season
And its leaf does not wither;
And in whatever he does, he prospers. (Ps 1:1–3)[10]

According to the psalmist, the one who avoids sin, sinful people, and sinful advisors and, instead, delights *in* and meditates *on* God, God's law, and God's advising is blessed and marked by focus, stability, nourishment, productivity, sustainability, and prosperity. James echoes Psalm 1 in his declaration of the objective value of living a Scripture-shaped life.

Conversely, God's people who hear matters of God's will—thereby thwarting any possible claim of ignorance of his expectations and invitations—and do not seek to live lives aligned with God's will, are described by James as being deluded.[11] Failure to apply God's word to life is self-harm. God's people are to apply God's word to their lives (i.e., to become increasingly and progressively Christlike by the power of the Holy Spirit) for his glory and for their own good, as intended by God.

The Lord Jesus offered a similar warning to the people of Israel during the early stages of his earthly ministry when, coming to the end of the Sermon on the Mount, he said:

Therefore everyone who hears these words of Mine and acts on them, may be compared to a wise man who built his house on the rock. And the rain fell, and the floods came, and the winds blew and slammed against that house; and yet it did not fall, for it had been founded on the rock. Everyone who hears these words of Mine and does not act on them, will be like a foolish man who built his house on the sand. The rain fell, and the floods came, and the winds blew and slammed against that house; and it fell—and great was its fall. (Matt 7:24–27)

Like James after him, Jesus was calling for an immediate and intentional response to his teaching, inviting his hearers to "build a solid foundation that combine[d] authentic commitment to Christ with persevering obedience."[12] The Lord wanted everyone who heard his words to act on

10. Consider also Jesus's words in Luke 11:28: "But [Jesus] said, 'On the contrary, blessed are those who hear the word of God and observe it.'"

11. See also Col 2:4. With a scan of the New Testament one may add that these deluded individuals are also neglectful (Heb 13:2, 16) and, ultimately, unblessed (e.g., Eph 6:1–3).

12. Blomberg, *Matthew*, 134.

them. His desire was for his hearers to be not only understanders or comprehenders, but doers[13] as application would bring stability while negligence would bring calamity. To remain merely hearers of God's word and not doers is dangerous, irresponsible, and irreverent. For God's people to be kept from applying God's word, aligning their lives with the revealed will of God, is to keep them, as James said, in a state of delusion, and as Jesus said, living lives of instability, and as they both said, in a state of deficient blessing.

As was briefly mentioned regarding the words of James, the nature of Scripture itself demands its applicability as does at least one of its self-stated goals, that is, the conformation of the people of God into the image of the Son of God (Rom 8:29; 1 Cor 15:49; 2 Cor 3:18; Col 3:10). Paul, after reminding Timothy of the essence of the word—"All Scripture is inspired by God"—immediately describes the usefulness of the word—"and profitable for teaching, for reproof, for correction, for training in righteousness; so that the man of God may be adequate, equipped for every good work" (2 Tim 3:16–17). The goal of Scripture is to equip the people of God for all they are to do for God in this world and it is able to accomplish that goal because it is God-breathed. As another has stated, "the basis of its profitableness lies in its inspired character."[14]

The testimony of Scripture is clear: God's word was given not to merely fill minds but to transform lives[15] and is uniquely and perfectly capable of accomplishing that end. Whether those sitting at the feet of the Master himself, those listening to James's epistle being read aloud for the first time, or the members of the church down the street today, God's people are called to put God's word into practice for their own good, for the good of those around them, and for the glory of him who has spoken. There are blessings associated with obedient, Spirit-empowered alignment with God's revealed will, and there are dangers associated with failure to do so.

---

13. Certainly, understanding God's word is a necessary step *toward* its application, but it is not application itself. In the same way, conviction under the word of God is not application, but can serve as fuel propelling God's people toward application. The task of the preacher, then, is to publicly showcase God's word to God's people that they may understand what the author is *doing* with what he is saying, facilitate Spirit-wrought conviction, and lead the flock in the direction of the divinely intended application of that specific pericope of Scripture (i.e., the *divine demand* of the text). More on this in chapter 2.

14. Guthrie, *Pastoral Epistles*, 164.

15. Even a simple study of οὖν ("therefore") in New Testament epistolary literature reveals the prevalence of calls to action rooted in truths taught (e.g., Rom 6:1, 15, 12; 12:1–2; 13:12; 14:13, 16; 1 Cor 4:16; 11:20–21; 16:11, 18; 2 Cor 7:1; 8:24; Gal 5:1; Eph 4:1, 17; 5:1, 7, 15; 6:14; Phil 3:15; Col 2:6; 3:1, 5, 12; 2 Tim 1:8; Heb 4:11, 14; 10:19; Jas 4:7; 5:7, 16; 5:6; 2 Pet 4:1, 7; 5:6; 2 Pet 3:17; 3 John 8).

It is with the above realities in mind that it can be stated that part of a pastor's divine job description (i.e., a facet of what it means to faithfully "preach the word") is to aid God's people in the *doing* of what it is they are *hearing*. Stated otherwise, if pastors are called to feed God's people from God's word, and God's people are called to apply God's word, then it is incumbent upon pastors to lovingly aid God's people in that process, helping individual believers (and the corporate body of believers together) understand the applicability of biblical truth, empowering them to walk in said truth, and thereby experience the blessings promised by God for doing so. For a pastor to stop short of application in preaching is for him to prepare a healthy expositional meal for the sheep providentially placed under his care yet risk keeping it out of their reach, enjoyment, and nourishment. As one homiletician has aptly written,

> [The] preaching of Scripture is not for the purpose of imparting information, but for transforming people by the power of the Holy Spirit—the changing of lives to conform to the image of Christ, by the instrumentality of God's word. Week by week, sermon by sermon, pericope by pericope, habits are changed, dispositions are created, character is built, and the image of Christ is formed.[16]

The preacher, as shepherd of God's people, therefore, must not only *read* the biblical text (e.g., Neh 8:1–3; 1 Tim 4:13) and *explain* the biblical text (e.g., Neh 8:4–8; 1 Tim 4:11; 6:2), he must also help hearers *apply* the biblical text to their lives for the purpose of spiritual maturation (e.g., Neh 8:9–12; 1 Tim 5:7; 6:17; 2 Tim 3:16–17),[17] the *telos* for which the word was given.[18]

16. Kuruvilla, *Privilege the Text!*, 268. "Pericope" will be used here, as in Kuruvilla's work, to describe a segment of the Scriptures used in preaching and worship within the context of a local body of believers. "['Pericope'] refers to a portion of the biblical text that is of manageable size for homiletical and liturgical use in an ecclesial setting." Kuruvilla, *Privilege the Text!*, 91.

17. A note regarding *specificity* of application is appropriate here. Because preaching is done by a *particular* shepherd given by God to a *particular* people, the application of any pericope in any sermon should be precise, not vague, specific, not general. The way in which any given application is presented should be uniquely tailored to the congregation for which it has been prayerfully crafted. This specificity of application, obviously, grows out of a pericopal theology that is consistent across continents and eras.

18. "Application is thus an indispensable component of preaching; indeed, it is its endpoint: preaching cannot be reckoned complete without application. Without application, the field of homiletics lies fallow, preaching unproductive, and the sermon stillborn . . . Only in personal application does the text accomplish its meaning." Kuruvilla, *Privilege the Text!*, 135–36. Also, "The use of application in exposition is an integral element of exposition. It is important that the application is bound to the exegetical discovery of the text at hand and directed to personal response . . . What makes

AN OBSTACLE TO THE WORD APPLIED IN PREACHING

But how is the application of the biblical text accomplished rightly, confidently, and responsibly today? It is obviously one matter to consider how the Lord Jesus and his apostles, inspired by the Holy Spirit as they were, made moves to relevant application for their hearers. It is another matter entirely for a preacher today to do the same. It is one thing for the apostle Paul to say with all conviction and the full weight of divine authority, "Therefore . . . !" It is altogether another for Rev. Dale E. Bread to call for the same level of hearer compliance and urgency.

The difference between the two is rooted in the certainty of the former that the call for application of the speaker is the same as the call for application of the source (i.e., God himself). To experience this consistency, the divine demand[19] of any given text must be identified, communicated, and used as the essential foundation on top of which valid application can be built with confidence. It is only with the intended application of the biblical author growing out of the divine demand of the word of God that any contemporary communicator can wield such authority.

If the divine demand of any pericope of Scripture must be identified for valid application to be declared with authority, the distinction between authorial *sayings* and *doings* must first be understood. This is true for all communication, written or otherwise. For example, if a mother says to her daughter, "The door is open," she has used specific words, grammar, and syntax in her communique. These constitute what the mother is *saying* and must be understood if the maternal demand is to be realized and, eventually, applied rightly by the daughter. However, understanding what Mom is saying is not enough. Rather, a grasp of what she is *doing* with what she is saying is essential for right application and maternal favor. Is the statement of an open door an invitation for company (i.e., an "open door policy")? Is it Mom's way of asking her daughter to leave? Or does the mother want her child to close a door that has been mistakenly left ajar? If the daughter misses the *doings*, regardless of her understanding of the *sayings*, there is a much lower possibility of her comprehending the maternal demand and, thus, applying her mother's words in a way that satisfies.

---

preaching powerful is an implicit trust in the authenticity and nature of the Scriptures, faithfulness to the text, and a life that reflects the convictions." Hargrove, "Implication and Application in Exposition," 91.

19. This work will use the language of Kuruvilla in describing the intended weight of any given text: "[The] divine demand is the gracious call of a loving Father to his children to align their lives with the precepts, priorities, and practices of his ideal world . . . [E]ach text bears a divine demand intended to be obeyed, not as a condition for salvation, but as a call to sanctification." Kuruvilla, *Privilege the Text!*, 152, 211.

To use a biblical example, suppose a local pastor decides to preach this coming Sunday on the opening chapter of Jonah. In this scene, the prophet runs away from God's assignment to bring a message of judgement to the city of Nineveh and, instead, boards a ship headed in the opposite direction. God, however, sends a storm upon the sea so vicious that it strikes fear in the hearts of the seasoned mariners on board. They all call out to their gods for relief and mercy but to no avail. It is only when Jonah is discovered as being the catalyst for the tempest and is thrown overboard that the storm calms, the ship sails on, and the prophet sinks.

The pastor, a faithful shepherd of God's flock, reads the narrative with enthusiasm. He then explains the passage, describing Assyria's wickedness and their tenuous relationship with Israel, illustrating the geography of Jonah's attempted escape, and parsing out and comparing the reactions to the divine storm of both the prophet and the pagans. There is no doubt that the people in the pews have now heard and understood the passage. But how can this faithful shepherd help his flock *do* what they have now *heard*? And, more than that, how can the specific application he offers be done with conviction rooted in confidence that he is accurately mirroring the intended application of the Holy Spirit working through the human author and, thus, wielding divine authority? Can this pastor declare, "As God's people today, we must not run from God"? What about, "We must, even this week, seek ways to be faithful witnesses to unbelievers around us"? Or, "Today, we can see the storms of life as possible correctives from God to our not-so-hidden acts of disobedience"? Are these *all* valid moves to application from Jonah 1?[20] Are these all examples of God-pleasing *doings* with the textual *sayings*? If so, one has to wonder whether potential applications from any given text are only limited by the creativity and imagination of the preacher. If not, which is/are valid and why? If all are not in line with God's intended application, then not all carry the weight and authority of God.

T. David Gordon, while not referring to the application of God's word *per se*, identifies a significant and foundational issue when he writes, "If the hearer's duty in listening to a sermon is to be willing to submit one's will to God's will, then one can only do this if the preacher does his duty of demonstrating that what he is saying is God's will."[21] Not just any explanation of divine *doings* will do because not just any explanation of divine *doings* is accurate. Similarly, and by extension, not just any suggestion of application

---

20. Again, it should be noted that, while these general statements of application are useful for a discussion like this, in the act of preaching, specificity is necessary. A particular shepherd must help his hearers apply the theology of the pericope with an exactness that the above examples do not allow in their vagueness.

21. Gordon, *Why Johnny Can't Preach*, 18.

will do because not just any suggestion of application carries with it the authoritative weight of God's will. In fact, only the suggested application that is in line with God's intended application is binding on the lives of God's people. Gordon continues, "the minister is only to be obeyed insofar as he demonstrates to the hearer what God's will is."[22] As the authority of God's appointed shepherd (i.e., messenger) is only that of delegated authority from God and his word (i.e., Sender), the pastor must ensure that all facets of his preaching—application included—accurately reflect the intention of the segment of the word being preached.

Consider another biblical example, this time the genealogy that opens the New Testament. If it is true that "all Scripture is inspired by God and profitable" (2 Tim 3:16), then Matthew's list of ancient names is both inspired and profitable as well. As such, God's people are actually deficient (i.e., lacking something necessary for being "equipped for every good work" [2 Tim 3:17]) until they submit themselves to the breathed-out words of Matthew 1:1–17. To suggest this is not so would be to suggest that either (a) God inspired a portion of Scripture that is not necessary or (b) he gave us a passage that is not applicable, both of which contradict what Scripture itself communicates. Therefore, even Matthew's introductory genealogical record was intentionally included by God and inherently includes a "therefore" call to action to which God's people must adhere for his glory and for their own good.

But what is that call to action? What is the valid application of Matthew 1:1–17? How can a pastor confidently provide the people of God with a heart-arresting, conviction-shaping, action-demanding application that carries with it the weight of the authority of God? One need only scan the internet for sermons delivered on this particular text (or any text, for that matter) to learn that suggested applications are not only varied but myriad in their variations! Again, we ask: Are they *all* valid? If so, how can that be? And, if they are not all valid, which are, and how can believers, longing to submit to and align their lives with God's will, discern the right from the misguided?

Expanding our consideration from Matthew's opening paragraphs to the responsibilities of the pastor as a whole—the call to "preach the word"—these questions become as daunting as they are pressing. How does a preacher responsibly, consistently, and authoritatively move from an

---

22. Gordon, *Why Johnny Can't Preach*, 19. The author here touches on another relevant issue that will be highlighted in this research. Not only must the preacher identify and communicate valid and divine-authority-wielding application to his hearers, but he also must demonstrate how it has been identified, substantiating his claim from the text itself.

ancient text to a modern congregation? How does he, rightly discerning the divine demand of a text of inspired Scripture, lay before his people an appropriately authoritative "Therefore . . . !"? Said another way, how does a pastor, week after week, publicly move from inspired Scripture to divine demand to concrete application? Thomas Long articulates well the frustratingly indescribable way in which this task is usually communicated *to* preachers and experienced *by* preachers:

> [Alert] biblical preachers have been aware for some time that there is a bit of deception, a touch of legerdemain, built into that classical text-to-sermon process. The preacher takes the text and puts it through the paces of a good exegetical process. The grammar of the text is analyzed, word studies are conducted, the probable Sitz im Leben is established, and so on. The handle is turned, the wheels spin, the gears mesh, and in the end out pops a reasonably secure version of what the text meant in its historical context or, to put it more bluntly, what the text used to mean . . . Now, so what? The exegesis yielded the information that Paul responded in such and such a way to a question in Corinth about meat offered to idols, a question that would never in a million years occur to anyone in Kingsport, Tennessee, or Fresno, California. So what? . . . The preacher is simply told that now the gap must be bridged from the history of the text to the urgency of the contemporary situation. It is presented as an obvious next step, a child's leap across a puddle, but the honest preacher knows that the distance between what the text used to mean and what the text may now mean yawns wide, and the leap seems difficult indeed.[23]

"So what?" indeed. And even if the preacher, by some acts of divine providence, finds his way to the other side of the homiletical puddle and is convicted of the specific applicability of a specific text they have uncovered, how does the hearer understand this? How is the congregation convinced of the validity of said application or must they simply trust the preacher? There must be a way to traverse this chasm with objectivity and not guesswork, with a jump of conviction and not a leap of faith, with a confident pump of the fist and not an insecure shrug of the shoulders.

---

23. Long, "Use of Scripture," 344.

EXPLORING A POTENTIAL WAY FORWARD

Buckets of ink have been spilled over the topics of preaching, exegesis, homiletics, and hermeneutics, out of which many potential solutions have been proposed for the Bible-to-theology move.[24] As Long laments, though, fewer have tackled the theology-to-application move, often leaving it in the realm of mystery.

However, one homiletician, Abraham Kuruvilla, has recently attempted to bridge this gap by articulating and demonstrating a methodology through which a preacher can, with confidence and clarity, lead the people of God from the inspired word to the intended, and thus binding, application.[25] In fact, Long is one of the many voices who offers an endorsement of the maiden work of this scholar:

> Rarely does one find such a clear, careful, and comprehensive description of the goals and methods of biblical theological hermeneutics as we have in this volume by Abe Kuruvilla. The fact that the discussion never loses touch with the urgent task of preaching makes this volume not only provocative but virtually unique in the field.[26]

The aim of the current work is this: to test and observe how Kuruvilla's methodology works in real time for both the preacher declaring God's word and the congregation receiving God's word. More pointedly, the goal is to explore the effectiveness of a specific theology (i.e., pericopal theology)[27] and a specific hermeneutic (i.e., christiconic)[28] for the identification, development, communication, and reception of biblically founded, theologically valid, and hearer-relevant application.

24. For examples of works that attempt to help preachers make this move, see Chapell, *Christ-Centered Preaching*; Cone, *Integrating Exegesis and Exposition*; Sunukjian, *Invitation to Biblical Preaching*; Marshall, *Beyond the Bible*; Greidanus, *Modern Preacher and Ancient Text*; Robinson, *Biblical Preaching*; Johnson, *Glory of Preaching*; Stott, *I Believe in Preaching*.

25. Kuruvilla, *Privilege the Text!*

26. Thomas Long, cover endorsement for Kuruvilla, *Privilege the Text!*

27. This refers to the theology specific to a particular pericope, which functions as the pivotal bridge from an authoritative and ancient text to a modern and relevant application. See Kuruvilla, *Privilege the Text!*, 112–13.

28. A method of Bible interpretation that understands each pericope of Scripture to be placing divine demands upon contemporary believers, the summation of which provides a picture of Christlikeness, the Son being the only one to perfectly meet all of God's demands without sin (2 Cor 5:21; Heb 4:15; 7:26). Thus, for a believer to submit to the divine demand of each section of Scripture is to take obedient steps forward in the process of sanctification. See Kuruvilla, *Privilege the Text!*, 29–30.

Following the example of Kuruvilla,[29] a theological commentary for preachers was developed for the book of Jonah and was field-tested at Oakridge Bible Chapel (OBC) in Oakville, Ontario, Canada, in a four-week expository sermon series. In order to assess the effectiveness of pericopal theology and a christiconic hermeneutic in communicating both the divine demands and authoritative applications of the four pericopes of Jonah for God's people today, evaluation had to take place. To this end, a self-administered pretest and posttest survey was developed and distributed to volunteer participants from the congregation.[30] The tool focused on both the content of the book of Jonah (i.e., what God is *saying*) as well as the applicational weight of the book (i.e., what God is *doing* with what he is saying and wants his people to do in response). The intention was to observe and measure whether God's people who sat under God's word being preached in a way that emphasized and showcased both would likewise grow in their understanding of what God is both *saying* and *doing* in the text of Jonah. As a result, God's people would be understanding the divine demand of the text and the valid application it placed upon their lives.

Chapter 2 of this work discusses the theoretical, biblical, and theological basis for this project. This chapter will explore in more detail the vital role biblical preaching plays in corporate worship, the vital role application plays in biblical preaching, and what makes application valid. To flesh out the latter topic, Kuruvilla's pericopal theology and christiconic hermeneutic are explained and examined in detail as a proposed solution to the move-to-application obstacle.

Chapter 3 will build upon the previous chapter and provide the rationale for the current study. Atop the theoretical, biblical, and theological foundation for this project, this chapter will present the scaffolding upon which the research was built (i.e., the research question that both fueled and guided the study: Can a developed theological commentary for preachers based on pericopal theology and christiconic hermeneutic aid in the preacher's development of valid application and the comprehension thereof by the hearers?). In more detail than is allowed for here, chapter 3 will articulate the reason and process of the development of the pretest and posttest survey that was used to seek an answer to the above question as well as the process of its administration and evaluation.

---

29. See Kuruvilla, *Mark*; *Genesis*; *Ephesians*; *Judges*; and *1–2 Timothy, Titus*.

30. Through word-of-mouth advertisement of some members of OBC, eight Christians attending other churches participated as well (12 percent of all participants). Though not present for the sermon series, these participants listened to the sermon audio recordings or watched the sermon videos online instead. This will be noted in the section of this work that describes and discusses methodology.

The fourth chapter of this work will posit the answers to the proposed research question as allowed for by the collected data. The results of the collected pretest and posttest surveys are analyzed to form the basis for answering this question, addressing stated hypotheses, and are presented in detail.

Chapter 5 discusses what generalizations can be learned from this particular work that apply to the broader field of homiletics, hermeneutics, and pastoral ministry. This chapter is really the application of this work on finding application! Here some of the potentially significant implications of this project will be offered as well as the identification of other potential research questions that arise from this study that warrant further investigation and work.

2

Orientation to the Literature

PREACHING CHARACTERIZED BY FAITHFULNESS and clarity in its theology and in its applicability is immeasurably important to the health and spiritual growth of any local church and its individual congregants. Why? Because the word of God (what should be the foundation, content, and motivation for biblical preaching) was given for the progressive conformation of the lives of the people of God into the image of the Son of God by the power of the Spirit of God to the glory of God (Rom 8:4; 15:4; 1 Cor 15:40–49; 2 Cor 1:20; Phil 3:21; 2 Tim 3:16–17). It is a supernatural endeavor, supernaturally empowered, with a supernatural goal. Thus, of all the words that can be used to describe the act of preaching, *reverence* must be one of them.

In the Scriptures, by the Spirit, and through faith, God's people have been given all they need "pertaining to life and godliness" (2 Pet 1:3). God's people have been called to "be holy . . . in all [their] behavior" (1 Pet 1:15) and possess the necessary tools in God's word for this pursuit. Thus, it is important not only that God's people understand what God has provided (i.e., what he has *said*) but that they also understand how what he has provided should change their lives (i.e., what he desires them to *do* with what he has said). The application of biblical truth to the believer's life is crucial for the life of godliness and, because it is, it is also crucial for those handling God's word in front of God's people to be competent in providing biblically faithful and justifiable calls to action from any given passage of Holy Writ. Preaching, ideally done, must strive to be *relevant* just as it is *reverent*.

The purpose of what follows is to provide a summary of the current literature related to the areas of the development and the communication of valid application of an ancient text—God's *word*—to a modern audience —God's *people*—and, in so doing, provide the context for the current research. To ensure the structure being built is sturdy, we will begin by drilling deep into the bedrock of the necessity of preaching in corporate worship,[1] the necessity of application in preaching, and the necessity of validity in application. Only after these foundational pieces are securely and sequentially in place will methodology for obtaining applicational validity be addressed.

A VITAL COMPONENT TO CORPORATE WORSHIP: BIBLICAL PREACHING

The regular, physical gathering of God's people in community is vital for the Christian life and when truncated in any way, invariably produces truncated Christians (i.e., believers who are immature, carnal, undiscerning, undisciplined, etc).[2] But what are God's people to do together when they gather so as to avoid this diminishment? Is merely sharing the same space for an arbitrary period of time sufficient to that end or does Scripture itself give guidance on what elements, actions, and activities are to be involved when the body assembles? Is there a divinely established *sine qua non* of corporate worship, a list of God-given requirements without which the assembling of God's people ceases to fully *be* and *do* what it is supposed to *be* and *do*?

While many scholars and churchmen, both contemporary and historical, have attempted to compile such a list, consensus has not yet been realized. Some posit four non-negotiable elements while others offer seven, nine, or more.[3] However, it does not follow that a lack of harmony in the

1. One could, of course, drill the foundation deeper still and consider the necessity of corporate worship in the life of each believer. However, for the purposes of this work, the necessity of the gathering of God's people will be largely assumed.

2. Scripture clearly asserts that parts of the body (i.e., individual Christians) cannot function properly apart from the whole (i.e., the church) (1 Cor 12:14–20), and any declaration of member independence is short-sighted and foolish. Not only can the parts not exist without the whole, but they are each meticulously placed by an all-knowing and all-powerful God, according to his pleasure, to serve a specific function that benefits the body *in toto* and then, by extension, each facet individually.

3. In fact, a simple internet search for "essential elements of corporate worship" yields an illustrative variety. For a (small) sample, see Reiland, "5 Essential Elements Needed as We Reinvent Church," https://outreachmagazine.com/features/leadership/58883–5-essential-elements-needed-as-we-reinvent-church.html; Autry, "Giving Is An Essential Part of Corporate Worship," https://scottautry.com/2016/03/14/giving-is-an-essential-part-of-corporate-worship; Deeter, "7 Principles for Corporate Worship," https://www.

number of required elements for ideal Christian worship means total dis-
unity on each individual required element. To the contrary, there are a
handful of activities that are near-universally agreed upon as divinely appointed marks of Christian corporate life, one of which is the preaching and
teaching of God's word to God's people (2 Tim 34:2).[4]

As Haddon Robinson has said, "Preaching and teaching, of course, are
not the only means by which God builds His people, but they are His major
means."[5] It is to this end that God saw fit to assign certain individuals to this
task for the purpose of their listener's maturation, stability, unity, and holiness:

> And He gave some as apostles, and some as prophets, and
> some as evangelists, and some as pastors and teachers, for the
> equipping of the saints for the work of service, to the building
> up of the body of Christ; until we all attain to the unity of the
> faith, and of the knowledge of the Son of God, to a mature
> man, to the measure of the stature which belongs to the full-
> ness of Christ. As a result, we are no longer to be children,
> tossed here and there by waves and carried about by every
> wind of doctrine, by the trickery of men, by craftiness in de-
> ceitful scheming; but speaking the truth in love, we are to grow
> up in all aspects into Him who is the head, even Christ, from
> whom the whole body, being fitted and held together by what
> every joint supplies, according to the proper working of each
> individual part, causes the growth of the body for the building
> up of itself in love. (Eph 4:11–16)

An Example from the Old Testament

The impact of the public proclamation of the Scriptures upon the corporate
assembly of God's people is illustrated with profundity in the eighth chapter of Nehemiah.[6] After returning from a divinely prescribed and overseen

---

justindeeter.com/articles/archives/1739; Allen, "The Four Biblical Marks of Corporate
Worship," https://jasonkallen.com/2014/02/four-biblical-marks-corporate-worship.

4. Others may include the public reading of Scripture (1 Tim 4:13); the singing of
psalms, hymns, and spiritual songs (Eph 5:19; Col 3:16); and corporate prayer (1 Tim
2:1). Some will demand the inclusion of the observance of the ordinances—baptism
and the Lord's Supper—though the regularity with which these are experienced in the
gathering will vary, whereas the former three are done each time the church is together.

5. Robinson, "What Is Expository Preaching?," 59.

6. In fact, that the people of God together as a community is in focus is evidenced
by the noteworthy concentration of its reference (thirteen times) in the opening twelve
verses of Nehemiah 8.

disciplinary exile in Babylon (Nehemiah 1–2), and after refortifying the city of Jerusalem (Nehemiah 3–7), "all the people gathered as one man . . . and they asked Ezra the priest and scribe to bring the book of the law of Moses which the Lord had given to Israel" (v. 1).

> The people already respected the law of Moses and recognized its authority for their community. It is significant that this reading of the law and the worship service were not centered in the temple and not controlled by the priesthood. From this time on in Judaism, the Torah was more important than the temple. Likewise, for Christians, the living power of the Bible should be more important than any church building. Through Scripture the Holy Spirit brings people to abundant life.[7]

Ezra quickly accommodated the people's request (v. 3). The book of the law was read, translated, and explained for the people gathered "so that they understood the reading" (v. 8). In other words, the Scriptures were exposited as well as heard. And what was the response to the proclamation of God's word? "Then Nehemiah, who was the governor, and Ezra the priest and scribe, and the Levites who taught the people said to all the people, 'This day is holy to the Lord your God; do not mourn or weep.' For all the people were weeping when they heard the words of the law" (v. 9). Fueled by repentance for prior disobedience and a subsequent understanding of God's mercy, provision, and comfort (2 Kgs 22:11–13, 19), God's people experienced the dramatic power of God's word to transform lives by calling them back in line with God's will.[8]

The example of Ezra is but one of many Old Testament allusions to the practice, power, efficacy, and necessity of God's word, law, and works being proclaimed and explained to God's people,[9] a concept that continues to flower and crystallize in the New Testament.

---

7. Breneman, *Ezra, Nehemiah, Esther*, 224.

8. Breneman, *Ezra, Nehemiah, Esther*, 226–27. "The powerful exposition of the Word of God can bring deep conviction of sin. Repentance, however, must not degenerate into a self-centered remorse but instead must elicit joy in God's forgiving goodness." Longman and Garland, eds., *1 Chronicles–Job*, 518.

9. For examples, see Lev 10:9–11; Deut 31:11; 33:10; Josh 24; 1 Kgs 17:17–24; 1 Chr 16:8–36; 2 Chr 17:7–9; Pss 96; 105; Isa 55:10–11; Jer 14:14 (a negative example); Luke 1:15–17 (John the Baptist's assignment as last of the Old Testament prophets). For a brief overview of the proclamation of God's Word in the Old Testament, see Maier, "'Preach the Word.'"

A Pattern Continued in the New Testament

The pattern of the public preaching of God's word to God's people continues seamlessly from the Old Testament to the New. While an exhaustive study of the available examples is both beyond the scope of this work and unnecessary for its goals, one from the life of the Lord Jesus Christ will suffice.

After recording the events surrounding Jesus's birth (1:5–2:20), his introduction to the world (2:21–52), the ministry of his forerunner (3:1–22), and his qualifications as Messiah (3:23–4:13), Luke describes the beginnings of the Lord's Spirit-empowered (4:14) public ministry with a statement of his general methodology and initial reception: "And he began teaching in their synagogues and was praised by all" (4:15). At the outset of his time in the Israeli spotlight, Jesus goes to where God's people gathered for worship, i.e., the synagogue, to teach them.

In the following verse, the biblical author narrows the focus of his pen from Jesus's general ministry methodology to a specific occurrence of said ministry. "And he came to Nazareth, where he had been brought up; and as was his custom, he entered the synagogue on the Sabbath, and stood up to read" (4:16). Luke again emphasizes that the public teaching of God's people when gathered to worship is Jesus's *modus operandi*, i.e., "his custom." But in what follows the reader is given a more detailed insight into what his Sabbath teaching sessions involved.

> And the book of the prophet Isaiah was handed to him. And he opened the book and found the place where it was written, "The Spirit of the Lord is upon me, because he anointed me to preach the gospel to the poor. He has sent me to proclaim release to the captives, and recovery of sight to the blind, to set free those who are oppressed, to proclaim the favorable year of the Lord." And he closed the book, gave it back to the attendant and sat down; and the eyes of all in the synagogue were fixed on him. And he began to say to them, "Today this Scripture has been fulfilled in your hearing." (4:17–21)

Following the accepted custom of his day, Jesus stood to publicly read a section of the Hebrew Bible and then, after finishing, sat down and explained that same portion for those gathered.[10] The parallels with the aforementioned scene from Nehemiah are not difficult to identify. This seated synagogue sermon "explicitly indicates the vital significance of preaching in the Sprit-anointed mission Jesus inaugurated."[11]

---

10. Walvoord and Zuck, eds., *Bible Knowledge Commentary*, 214.

11. Blythe, "Place of Preaching," 55.

From Nehemiah to Jesus, the task of the public proclamation of God's word continues its God-established trajectory into today's pulpits. Centuries ago, reformer Martin Luther declared, "The highest worship of God is the preaching of the Word; because thereby are praised and celebrated the name and the benefits of Christ."[12] Similarly, and more recently, Albert Mohler has written, "The preaching of the Word is central, irreducible, and nonnegotiable to authentic worship that pleases God."[13] Though separated by half of a millennia and a number of significant theological differences, both Luther and Mohler agree that it is the word faithfully preached that most consistently, accurately, and fully lifts high the second person of the Godhead,[14] guided and empowered by the third person of the Godhead, for the glory of the first person of the Godhead.[15] If corporate worship is vital to the life of the believer, and if the word of God is vital for acceptable worship, then the word preached is to be its crescendo. But what characteristics are vital for acceptable preaching?

Not All Preaching Is Created Equal

All around the world each week there are countless preachers delivering countless sermons to countless congregations. The unfortunate reality, however, is that not all sermons are created equal, not all messages necessitate submission from hearers, and not all messengers should be given attention. It is for this reason and others that Scripture calls for hearer discernment (2 Pet 2:1; 1 John 4:1–6). That God would warn his people to cling to his commandments with purpose and intentionality (Deut 12:32; Josh 1:7; Prov 30:6; Rev 22:18) assumes the human propensity to stray from, add to, or take away from his gospel, his words, and his will.[16] If no risk exists for the perversion and misuse of God's word, there is no need for the warning to avoid perversions and misuses of it.

The repeated rebuke of Old Testament false prophets, those people deceitfully parading deviant or obscure messages as divine truth (e.g., Isa 9:15; Jer 37:19; Lam 2:14; Ezek 13:1–23; Hos 9:7), was continued after the

12. Lawson, *Heroic Boldness of Martin Luther*, 26.

13. Beeke and Benge, eds., *Pulpit Aflame*, 61.

14. While agreeing with Luther and Mohler that faithful preaching exalts Jesus Christ, this work demonstrates a potential disagreement on *how* preaching exalts Jesus Christ.

15. For a more in-depth study of the important and necessary role preaching plays in the life of the church, see Griffiths, *Preaching in the New Testament*.

16. Obviously, this error can be made with ignorance as easily as it can be made with malice and intentionality. Bad sermons can be preached by well-meaning believers (this author included, to be sure!) as well as wool-wrapped wolves.

ascension of Christ. The apostle Paul warned churches to deal harshly with preachers who declared a gospel inconsistent with that which God had already revealed (2 Cor 11:4; Gal 1:8). He also instructed Timothy, a young shepherd, to beware of the temptation to soft-pedal, dumb down, or alter the gospel to make it more palatable and less offensive to hearers (2 Tim 4:3–4). Again, this warning insinuates and presupposes the risk and the reality of irresponsible, substandard, and inaccurate gospel declaration.

These are but a few examples demonstrating that as long as God has been speaking to humanity, there have been people—whether maliciously or ignorantly—perverting his perfect, sufficient, and effective words to the detriment of themselves and their hearers. Speaking to the modern manifestations of this devastating trend and the much-needed reactionary reform, John MacArthur writes:

> The church has had enough erratic, trendy, whimsical preachers who flip-flop depending on the tide of the mob. What is most needed now are spiritual men who remain totally steadfast in an unstable world and who know their priorities. We need ministers whose heads are clear of deceit, false teaching, and unorthodox notions. We need preachers who will courageously declare the whole counsel of God. How wearisome it must be to God to hear insipid, innocuous pabulum dribbled out of pulpits instead of His Word![17]

Similarly, Haddon Robinson summarizes the potential distraction facing all who fill a pulpit: "For some preachers . . . fads in communication become more stimulating than the message."[18] When the message (i.e., the word of God) becomes eclipsed or supplemented with anything—no matter how well intentioned, creative, innovative, or methodologically sound—its power is dampened and its truth distorted.

As has been shown, the preaching of the word of God is vital for corporate worship. However, just as corporate worship must take a specific, God-prescribed shape to be the full blessing it is meant to be, so too preaching must adhere to God's intention in order to be most effective and affective. To say it another way, just as God's people are not free to reinvent their corporate gatherings without the expectation of negative consequence, so too the preacher is not free to reinvent preaching without the expectation of unwanted—albeit often unseen for a while—negative ramifications.

---

17. MacArthur, *Ashamed of the Gospel*, 51.

18. Robinson, *Biblical Preaching*, 16.

Preaching as God Intended

As the nature and power of God's word has already been addressed, it should not surprise that the type of preaching that brings God glory and affects change in the lives of God's people is preaching unapologetically and tightly tethered to the text of Scripture. Anything less and anything that loosens or disconnects from this inspired anchor fails to be the type of word proclamation God himself intended for his people because it is in preaching the word that the preacher is most committed and subjected to the inspiration, authority, power, and sufficiency of the biblical text, seeking to unleash the full weight of the passage being explained (i.e., the thrust of the pericope in question) so that it strikes the people of God in the manner the author intended (i.e., the divine demand laid upon the hearers).[19]

Even the most faithful, godly preacher is fallible and even the most captivating orator in the pulpit is powerless when they are disconnected from God's message as revealed in God's word. For this reason, the kind of preaching that is worth the time and effort to listen to is preaching that privileges not the man in the pulpit but the book that rests upon it. "Our task [as preachers] is not to stand in front of the Bible text, but behind it, ensuring that *it is doing the talking*."[20] It is when the preacher lets the Bible speak for itself, clearly explaining God's word, discerning its intended meaning, and applying its rightly discerned divine demand that preaching becomes the vital component to corporate worship and to the life of the individual Christian that God intends it to be.

A VITAL COMPONENT OF BIBLICAL PREACHING: VALID APPLICATION

Of the countless definitions of preaching that have been offered through the decades, not many fail to at least mention the importance of application for the hearer. Certainly, rightly understanding and communicating the truths of the text is important. Indeed, one "cannot decide what a passage means to us unless first we have determined what the passage means."[21] Thus, faithful interpretation and explanation are necessary precursors to faithful

19. As Johnson has said, "expository preaching is not about getting a message out of the text; it is about inviting people into the text so that the text can do what only the text can do." *Glory of Preaching*, 58.

20. Lamb, *Preaching Matters*, 33. Emphasis added. Also, Ash: "God does not want to know what we think. He wants us to know what he thinks." *Priority of Preaching*, 35.

21. Robinson, *Biblical Preaching*, 90. Emphasis added.

application. But, as has already been discussed in this work, a sermon that exposits the text without applying the text is like a builder who erects the walls of a house but fails to set the roof atop them. The roof cannot stand without the walls, but the walls without the roof make for an incomplete and largely useless home. So it is with biblical preaching.[22] A sermon must move, somehow, beyond a simple "this means that" description of a passage and toward a "therefore we must" call to action.

In his book *Saying It Well*, Charles Swindoll tells the story of sitting under the preaching of a skilled Bible teacher who frequently concluded his sermons with the hope-filled exhortation, "Now, may the Lord apply this to our hearts and lives. Let's pray."[23] The speaker made no attempt to aid his hearers in fleshing out the practical implications of the passage he had just taught. Rather, deciding explanation was sufficient, he intentionally left the application of his exposition for the individual and the Spirit of God to sort out between themselves after the benediction.

Now, to be clear, the Holy Spirit *must* be relied on for the application of the word of God to the lives of the people of God (Rom 8:1–39).[24] He is its Author, and he is the effector of true sanctification (Rom 15:16; 1 Cor 6:11; Gal 5:16; 1 Thess 5:23; 2 Thess 2:13; Heb 9:14; 1 Pet 1:2). This is an important tension to note. While it is the work and power of the Spirit, the preacher is graciously invited to play a role in the feeding of the sheep and in their calling to the diligent and dependent pursuit of holiness (John 21:15–19; Acts 20:28; 1 Pet 5:1–3).[25]

Taking this stewardship seriously, an aspect of the preacher's task is the helping of the people of God to understand how the ancient text carries with it divine demands for their lives today. Expositing the biblical text without helping hearers apply the biblical text is not preaching. God's word was given to be applied to the lives of God's people by the power of God's Spirit

22. For example, consider the words of Thomas when he asserts, "Preaching is teaching *plus* application. To suggest that preaching is application is to overstate the case, but unless there is a 'so what?' component, it is something less than preaching." In Beeke and Benge, eds., *Pulpit Aflame*, 75.

23. Swindoll, *Saying It Well*, 201.

24. The role of the Holy Spirit in illuminating, convicting, and applying the word to the reader and/or hearer cannot be overstated. However, this subject is beyond the scope of the current work. For brief discussions, see Willimon, "Preaching"; Yong, "Proclamation in/of the Spirit"; Johnson, "Standing in the Mystery," in *Glory of Preaching*, 239–44; Lamb, "Biblical Preaching Must Be Relevant," in *Preaching Matters*, 109–21; Arthurs, "The Worlds of the Listener," in Gibson, ed., *Worlds of the Preacher*, 89–106; Haykin, "The Power of Preaching," in Beeke and Benge, eds., *Pulpit Aflame*, 131–41.

25. For an example of a preacher thinking through the tensions involved in the preaching endeavor, see Banting, *Take Up and Preach*, 5–6.

that they may become more like God's Son. For a shepherd of God's flock to lead those under his care to nourishment, protecting them from danger along the journey, but stopping short of helping them ingest the meal is malpractice. "Without genuine relevance there is no sermon."[26] As preaching is vital to corporate worship, so application is vital to faithful preaching.

Not All Applications Are Created Equal

In the same way that not all sermons are created equal, not all applications from a biblical text are valid—just as a passage can be misunderstood, so it can be misapplied. Indeed, the former all but guarantees the latter but in no way does the latter automatically arrive if the former is avoided. Discernment must be exercised by both the communicator and the hearer "to see whether these things [are] so" (Acts 17:11).

Making the need for careful discernment increasingly important is the reality that it is possible for a statement to be both biblical and invalid, particularly within the sermonic enterprise. There are occasions when an articulated understanding of a text preached, i.e., the thrust of the passage, and the application of that text offered, i.e., its divine demand, may be true biblically (what has been said is supported *somewhere* in the corpus of Scripture) without being true from the passage of Scripture in question. When this takes place, validity is sacrificed.

For example, imagine you are sitting in church one Sunday and the preacher makes the assertion, "This passage of Scripture teaches us that God-honoring marriages are to reflect the self-sacrificial nature of the relationship of Christ to his church." Being an educated and biblically literate church member, you may shout, "Amen! Preach, brother!" In fact, not many regenerate hearers would find reason for disagreement in the pastor's postulation.

However, imagine that now, having calmed down from your enthusiastic outburst of affirmation, you glance down at the church bulletin in your hand and notice that the preacher's passage for the morning's sermon is not Ephesians 5 but Genesis 2. Does that not change your reaction? It should! Not only does Genesis 2 not discuss self-sacrifice, but the sacrifice of the Son of God for the New Testament people of God was nowhere on the horizon of salvation history at that point of the biblical story. All of a sudden it becomes clear that the preacher has misinterpreted the passage, missing the thrust of the Genesis text, and instead imported preconceived theological conclusions onto a text that teaches something different (something that, because of the nature of Scripture itself, is as essential for the hearers'

---

26. Greidanus, *Modern Preacher and Ancient Text*, 157.

walk with God as it is now missing from that congregation![27]). Again, the statement itself is true—even biblically defensible!—but it simply is not an accurate explanation of the particular passage of Scripture from which the pastor has been preaching this morning and, thus, invalid and should be rejected. If indeed the goal is to let the word of God speak, the preacher must allow it to do just that.

If the accusation of invalidity seems overly harsh and dogmatic language to use for a possibly honest misinterpretation of a passage that ends up leading to biblical truth regardless, one must consider the implications of the alternative. To accept what this imaginary pastor has done as less than invalid is to affirm any interpretation from any passage of Scripture so long as it has some connection to the text—regardless of how tenuous—and finds its terminus in a claim that sounds generally biblical. In the example above, God did not say what the pastor said God said in the particular passage from which the pastor has claimed God said it. No amount of biblical or systematic theology and no amount of human creativity can change that reality, though it can camouflage the error. Thus, the stated authorially intended thrust of Genesis 2 is an invalid interpretation and should be labeled as such with the added acknowledgement that the preacher has robbed the congregation of the *right* interpretation of the text while, at the same time, feeding them the *wrong* one. It is the double-edged sword of hermeneutical and homiletical malpractice.[28]

The same error can, and does, take place with application as with interpretation. (In fact, as has been mentioned already and will be discussed later, there can be no valid application without, first, valid interpretation and, thus, the two are very much connected.) Imagine that now, having recovered from the pastoral misstep you witnessed the previous weekend, you are back at that same church the following Sunday morning for corporate worship. This time, the preacher seems to be on point. He is walking

---

27. "*All* Scripture is inspired by God and profitable . . ." (2 Tim 3:16, emphasis added). The implication is that Genesis 2, like Ephesians 5, is breathed out by God himself and useful—even necessary—for the edification of God's people. It also means that Genesis 2 is *different from* Ephesians 5. While they may both share ideas, e.g., marriage union, they are not interchangeable, nor should they be conflated.

It should also be mentioned that the above illustration assumes the sermon in question was not a topical sermon that included both Genesis 2 *and* Ephesians 5. While there may be a time and place for the responsible and prayerful use of such sermons, it is the conviction of this author that topical preaching is not the ideal diet for God's people. That said, a discussion on the potential benefits and liabilities of such preaching is beyond the scope of this work.

28. It is little wonder why James warned, "Let not many of you become teachers, my brethren, knowing that as such we will incur a stricter judgment" (3:1)!

through the Old Testament book of Jonah and as he comes to the end of his sermon he makes the move to application: "As God's people we must embrace the discomforts that accompany the Christian life and avoid the prioritization of earthly ease. Brothers and sisters, seek comfort in God, not in things!" According to the pastor, Jonah's inflated love of the day-old, shade-providing, comfort-securing plant that God provided for him (Jonah 4:6) and his embarrassing and revealing emotional breakdown at its worm-wrought demise (4:7–8) serves as a negative example for God's people throughout time and space. Stated simply, Christians today must not be like Jonah, prioritizing our own comfort and ease of life over all else. Instead, seek *comfort in God, not in things!*

Now to the task of determining whether or not the proposed application is one of validity. Is the admonition to avoid elevating the idol of personal comfort above all else biblical? Of course it is. Thus, the application suggested by the preacher is taught somewhere in the canon of Scripture (e.g., Matt 10:24–42; Mark 10:13–31; 14:1–11; 15:1–39; Luke 9:12–62; 2 Cor 1–18[29]). But is it taught in the book of Jonah and, thus, valid for *this* sermon from *this* text? Can the call to God's people to reject the idol of personal comfort be justified and rooted in the actual text of this minor prophet? The burden is upon the preacher to demonstrate that it can be and in this example he would probably be unsuccessful in doing so. While on the first week you attended the pastor declared a good truth from the wrong text, the second week has found him laying a good application from the wrong text. In both cases, both moves are invalid.

Once again, if this seems hyperbolic and unnecessarily polemic, the implications of anything less must be considered. If any application is valid from any passage so long as it shares commonalities with the text and is supported from somewhere else in the canon, then is the preacher's imagination and creativity the only real restriction on the development of application? Could that same pastor have called his congregation to a vegan lifestyle based upon God's use of animals to teach lessons? What about charging them to shorten their evangelistic appeals to no more than five words since that was all Jonah needed when he finally arrived in Nineveh?[30]

---

29. While all of these passages (and many others) teach facets of the sacrificial nature of discipleship, they all provide a unique facet of that call. Thus, they are not being listed as if to indicate a uniform teaching. Rather, they are illustrative to the point that what this hypothetical pastor was communicating may have been better supported by another text from another biblical book.

30. "'Yet forty days and Nineveh will be overthrown.' Then the people of Nineveh believed in God" (3:4b–5a). The Hebrew version of Jonah's sermon is five words: עוֹד אַרְבָּעִים יוֹם וְנִינְוֵה נֶהְפָּכֶת.

If those two suggestions sound nonsensical, an introspective reader must ask himself, "Why?" What makes the applications of anti-meat and anti-verbosity less valid than anti-comfort? If there is no right interpretation, all interpretations are potentially right. Likewise, if there is no right thrust of a text leading to right divine demand leading to right application, then all suggested demands and subsequent applications are potentially valid.

It has been said that "All good theology is intensely practical."[31] But it is also true that all good theology must first be intensely biblical even before it can be intensely practical. A preacher's theology (i.e., his explanations of what a biblical author is *saying* and *doing*) must be rooted *in* the text and defensible *by* the text. Only when this is properly understood can the preacher move to implications and applications of that specific text, rooted in the theology of the text, to the lives of the hearers. If these steps are swapped, softened, or side-stepped, validity crumbles in either interpretation or application, or both. Thus, while application is a vital component of faithful, biblical preaching, not all application is created equal because not all application is valid.

As has been illustrated above, the discernment and articulation of valid application from particular passages of Scripture is as difficult as it is crucial. One author has gone so far as labeling the development of valid application "one of the most demanding intellectual tasks imaginable . . . Anyone who proclaims how easy it is . . . is probably prevaricating, or is very bad at the task, or is so very experienced at it as to have forgotten the intellectual and spiritual task that it is."[32] But the difficulty of the task does not negate its necessity; in fact, it may serve to highlight it. If God's people are going to be brought progressively into alignment with God's will for them as individuals (i.e., sanctification) and as a church, the movement from text to praxis must take place.[33] Valid application must be sought, dug for, examined, tested, and clung to.

31. Kreider, *God with Us*, 33.

32. Porter, "Hermeneutics, Biblical Interpretation, and Theology," in Marshall, *Beyond the Bible*, 121.

33. Kuruvilla, *Vision for Preaching*, 113. Few would consider it faithful preaching if a pastor simply stood in the pulpit, read a psalm, and sat back down. Why? Because preaching requires more than simply reading the text. It includes explanation of the text. So too with application. Just as *reading* the passage is not sufficient for faithful preaching, so also *reading* and *explaining* are not sufficient. Application must be specified and communicated to the particular congregation for which the preaching is prepared.

O Application, O Application, Wherefore Art Thou Application?

Having established the significance of this step in the homiletical process begs the obvious question: How is an expositor and, by extension, the hearer to responsibly move from an ancient text (i.e., the then) to a modern, valid application (i.e., the now)? Is the applicability of biblical texts subjective (i.e., "to each their own"), the implication being that all suggestions are equally valid? Or did the Author of Scripture have something more specific in mind and if so, how does one uncover those specifics and communicate them clearly and with relevance? Is the move from text to praxis some sort of magical, fingers-crossed jump in which the preacher hopes and prays he will land on faithful ground? Can a member of a congregation evaluate and discern pastoral calls to action, testing their validity instead of simply taking the expert's word for it? Is there an objectivity to the identification, articulation, communication, and reception of the application of any given passage of Scripture?

The difficulty of the move from interpretation to valid application, as well as the need for more research in this area, is illustrated by a quick glance across the field of biblical hermeneutics and homiletics and the collective understanding of the preaching task. Consider the handful of definitions below taken from some of the most well-known and well-respected practitioners and thinkers on the subject.

> The message [of an expository sermon] finds its sole source in Scripture. The message is extracted from Scripture through careful exegesis. The message preparation correctly interprets Scripture in its normal sense and its context. The message clearly explains the original God-intended meaning of Scripture. The message applies the Scriptural meaning for today.[34]

> Expository preaching is that preaching which takes for the point of a sermon the point of a particular passage of Scripture. That's it.[35]

> Expository preaching is the communication of a biblical concept derived from and transmitted through a historical-grammatical and literary study of a passage in its context, which the Holy Spirit first applies to the personality and experience of the preacher then through him to hearers.[36]

---

34. Mayhue, "Rediscovering Expository Preaching," in MacArthur, *Preaching*, 12–13.

35. Dever, *Nine Marks of a Healthy Church*, 40.

36. Robinson, *Biblical Preaching*, 20.

Expository preaching is the Spirit-empowered explanation and proclamation of the text of God's Word with due regard to the historical, contextual, grammatical, and doctrinal significance of the given passage, with the specific object of invoking a Christ-transforming response.[37]

Preaching is theology coming through a man who is on fire . . . What is the chief end of preaching? I like to think it is this. It is to give men and women a sense of God and his presence.[38]

Exposition refers to the content of the sermon (biblical truth) rather than its style (a running commentary). To expound Scripture is to bring out of the text what is there and expose it to view. The expositor opens what appears to be closed, makes plain what is obscure, unravels what is knotted, and unfolds what is tightly packed.[39]

An expository sermon may be defined as a message whose structure and thought are derived from a biblical text, that covers the scope of the text, and that explains the features and context of the text in order to disclose the enduring principles for faithful thinking, living, and worship intended by the Spirit, who inspired the text.[40]

[To preach is] to rightly interpret and explain the text, in its context, and to bring the text to bear upon the lives of the congregants.[41]

Expository preaching grounds the message in the text so that all the sermon's points are the points in the text, and it majors in the texts's major ideas. It aligns the interpretation of the text with the doctrinal truths of the rest of the Bible (being sensitive to systematic theology). And it always situates the passage within the Bible's narrative, showing how Christ is the final fulfillment of the text's theme (being sensitive to biblical theology).[42]

37. Olford and Olford, *Anointed Expository Preaching*, 69.
38. Lloyd-Jones, *Preaching & Preachers*, 110–11.
39. Stott, *Between Two Worlds*, 125–26.
40. Chapell, *Christ-Centered Preaching*, 31.
41. Allen, *Letters to My Students*, 38.
42. Keller, *Preaching*, 32.

. . . the preacher's task is . . . to present the true and exact meaning of the biblical text . . . in a manner that is relevant to the contemporary listener.[43]

[Expository preaching is] unfolding the text of Scripture in such a way that makes contact with the listener's world while exalting Christ and confronting them with the need for action.[44]

Expositional preaching is preaching in which the main point of the biblical text being considered becomes the main point of the sermon being preached.[45]

As the sample above demonstrates, most articulations of the purpose and path of preaching share common elements. Many acknowledge, in some way, the role of the Holy Spirit in the process. Similarly, most name the source of the content of the sermon as "the word of God," "the text," "Scripture," or "the Bible." The message of the sermon given must be "grounded in," "aligned with," or "derived from" the special revelation of God.

Another scan of the provided definitions above reveals a near-universal attempt to describe the move from the word of God to the truth to be presented to the hearers. This is the interpretation process being articulated. Words used to describe this effort include "grammatical," "structure," "expose," "historical," "contextual," "extraction," "unfold," and "God-intended meaning," with the process being called "careful," "exactly," "clearly," and "correctly." Evidently, the move from the biblical text to theology is important enough to demand attention from these homileticians as they define what it is that makes preaching *biblical* preaching. By definition, it must include a preacher moving from text to explanation, from Scripture to theology.

But what of the move from explanation to application, from theology to implication? How much attention is given, how much detail provided, how much space assigned to that movement? Below is a compilation of what the above definitions say about the role application plays in expository preaching.

- Invoke a Christ-transforming response
- Apply the scriptural meaning for today
- A biblical concept applied
- A sense of God and his presence

43. Sunukjian, *Invitation to Biblical Preaching*, 9–10.
44. Begg, *Preaching for God's Glory*, 23.
45. Dever and Gilbert, *Preach*, 36.

- Enduring principles for faithful thinking, living, and worship
- Relevant to the contemporary listener
- Makes contact with the listener's world . . . confronts with the need for action

If asked, those who penned the above definitions may agree that helping God's people apply God's word is somewhat important for the preacher. (For some it simply is not important enough to include in its definition. Thus, it would seem, that preaching can be faithful preaching even without application.) But even a quick glance reveals that there is far more specificity and objectivity in the explanation of interpretation than there is in that of application. In fact, it almost seems that, for those who mentioned it at all, application is an appendix to the dissertation of interpretation. It is the dessert served after a fine meal—nice and enjoyable if you have room to spare, but altogether unnecessary.

In this author's mind, the imbalance of attention in definitions like those provided and considered communicates one of two possible realities. First, the application of Scripture in preaching is deemed to be relatively unimportant when compared to interpretation. Space and attention are given to facets of preaching based on their perceived level of necessity to the task. Understanding the passage, digging into the context, covering the scope of the pericope, and communicating its God-intended meaning is primary. The move to application is a secondary and less crucial move. This is why less attention is given it.[46]

The second possible reason for the observed imbalance in the above definitions is that there is a dearth of understanding how to consistently apply the biblical text to modern hearers. It is not that the authors above think it an unimportant move at all; it is that they simply do not have a sharable plan in how to rightly and consistently arrive at that destination. Built atop mountains of research and thought on the movement from text to theology, there is much to say about its importance and significance to biblical preaching. Unfortunately, the same cannot be said for the move from theology to praxis.[47] This is why less attention is given it and why when attention is paid to application, it is typically vague and unhelpful.

46. This may, in fact, be true. However, even if the application of a biblical text is understood as less foundational than its explanation, i.e., portraying the textual thrust, this does not necessitate the unimportance of the former. Just because the walls of a building cannot stand without a solid foundation, and just because the foundation can exist without the walls, does not mean the walls are unimportant.

47. In addition to that, there exists today an abundance of resources, e.g., biblical commentaries, full of insights on what the biblical authors are *saying*, but far less

So, which is it? Is biblical application in faithful preaching not given as much attention as biblical interpretation because it is deemed less important or because it is less understood? Or perhaps the answer is a combination of the two. To attempt an answer to this question, one can read the entirety of the works from which the above definitions were lifted, and when this is done it becomes clear that the answer is not likely the former suggestion. In fact, in many of the widely read works on biblical preaching, there are chapters and sections dedicated to the importance of application.[48] Thus, it is difficult to conclude that, generally speaking, the modern homiletics community holds application as unimportant, though some may hold it as of lesser importance than interpretation.[49]

That leaves this author with one possible conclusion: The reason for the collective relative silence and methodological ambiguity on the issue of the development of valid application in biblical preaching is the collective uncertainty as to how it is accomplished with conviction and precision. Simply put: We do not know how to apply as well as we believe we know how to interpret. This was true in the 1980s, when Haddon Robinson lamented that "Many homileticians have not given accurate application the attention it deserves. No book has been published devoted exclusively, or even primarily, to the knotty problems raised by application. As a result, many church members having listened to orthodox sermons all their lives, may be practicing heretics."[50]

Like the explanation of electricity from an unlearned parent to an inquisitive child typically devolves into some version of "It just works, and I do not really know how," so it seems with preachers explaining the applicability of the biblical text: "It just applies, but we do not really know how." While

---

venturing to explore and articulate what they are *doing* with what they are saying, i.e., the move to valid application.

48. For examples see Sunukjian, "Form the Take-Home Truth," in *Invitation to Biblical Preaching*, 65–84; Beeke, "Part III: Preaching Experientially Today," in *Reformed Preaching*, 349–439; Chapell, "The Practice of Application," in *Christ-Centered Preaching*, 209–36; Johnson, "Walking the Sermon into Everyday Life: Implication and Application," in *The Glory of Preaching*, 158–71. Amazingly (and, perhaps, quite tellingly), in his groundbreaking work on biblical preaching, Haddon Robinson admits the importance of application but only dedicates a handful of pages to its discussion, a discussion that does not aid the preacher in the development of valid application. See Robinson, *Biblical Preaching*, 89–96.

49. Because a sermon that misses the mark in interpretation will almost certainly miss the mark in application (the latter grows out of the former), interpretation can be understood as holding a more primary role. However, if the goal of faithful preaching is that the people of God become increasingly like the Son of God, a false dilemma must be avoided, and both interpretation and application must be held as equally essential.

50. Robinson, *Biblical Preaching*, 89–90.

many are convinced that the Bible should be applied today, many are also unsure of how to consistently accomplish this task while ensuring validity. Recently, however, one scholar has set out to provide objectivity and clarity where there has seemed to be little for a while.

A Possible Explanation for Application Identification

> The Bible affirms that "whatever was written in former times was written for our instruction" (Rom 15:4). How exactly "our instruction" is accomplished is a question that has not been satisfactorily resolved. The challenge of bridging the gap between an ancient text and a modern audience, both culturally conditioned entities, is no doubt a burdensome one. On one side of this gap is the historical entity of the text; on the other, the existential situation of the community of God addressed from the pulpit . . . the crux of the hermeneutical problem is the traversal from the then of the text to the now of the audience; words written in an earlier age are to be transposed in some fashion across a divide into a later era.[51]

It is with the above statement that Abraham Kuruvilla begins his seminal work, *Privilege the Text!: A Theological Hermeneutic for Preaching*, setting course for the seemingly uncharted waters of sermonic application. Acknowledging that attempts have been made in the past to aid preachers with the move from text to praxis (e.g., the systematization and atomization of the biblical text),[52] Kuruvilla, while admitting their place, declares that all have been insufficient and largely unsuccessful at the task they were attempting. Instead, Kuruvilla suggests, only a theological hermeneutic committed to the privileging of the inspired text of Scripture can help preachers arrive at the desired destination. Not only does this provide a method of text-centered and testable interpretation, but from that interpretation is provided a method of developing application that is clearly supported by the passage of Scripture out of which it is claimed to have arisen.

In the pages that follow, Abraham Kuruvilla's proposed theology, hermeneutic, and method of interpretation will be briefly described.[53] What has been proposed by this homiletician is a suggested method of developing

---

51. Kuruvilla, *Privilege the Text!*, 19–20.

52. Kuruvilla, *Privilege the Text!*, 21–24.

53. Space does not permit, nor does this study necessitate, an in-depth description of the theology and hermeneutic proposed. For a more detailed and exhaustive treatment, see Kuruvilla, *Privilege the Text!*

valid application, which is vital to biblical preaching, which is vital to corporate worship, which is vital to the Christian life. Once Kuruvilla's work has been summarized, the remainder of this study will seek to test whether it accomplishes what it purposes to accomplish.

EN ROUTE TO VALID APPLICATION: PERICOPAL THEOLOGY

In order to arrive at valid application of a given biblical text, two movements must take place: (1) the preacher must move from the text to pericopal theology and (2) from the established theology to application.[54] It is the theology of the chosen preaching text (i.e., the theology of the pericope[55]) that bridges the chasm between the then and the now as it is rooted in that which is consistent and unchanging between the two: God himself (Mal 3:6). While cultural climate, geography, language, and original audiences are nearly always hurdles around which the expositor must maneuver when seeking to apply the ancient text to a modern audience, the consistency and predictability of Scripture's Author—his character, his plans, his purposes, etc.—makes the process not only possible but beautifully beneficial and worshipful. However, to accomplish the task of moving from ancient Scripture to modern congregation, a robust hermeneutic must be put in place. Without such a hermeneutic, subjectivity rules the day in both interpretation and application. Not only does this make it difficult for a preacher to be consistent in biblical interpretation, but it also fails to provide a reproducible model for the congregation to observe, learn, and adapt themselves.

Kuruvilla's pericopal theology attempts to fill that hermeneutical void and is founded on the assertion that authors are always "doing things with what they say" and that the text itself indicates its own thrust—its intended purpose—which must be identified and communicated in order for valid application to be proposed.[56] Without the former, there can be no latter.

For example, a mother and her teenage son are standing in the kitchen of their home when she turns to him and says, "The car is running." The semantic meaning of the statement (i.e., what the mother is *saying*) has to

54. Kuruvilla, *Privilege the Text!*, 90.

55. Kuruvilla, *Privilege the Text!*, 91. A pericope of Scripture "refers to a portion of the biblical text that is of manageable size for homiletical and liturgical use in an ecclesial setting . . . It is through pericopes, read and exposited in congregations as fundamental units of the scriptural texts, that the community of God corporately encounters the Bible."

56. Kuruvilla, "Pericopal Theology," 3–17.

do with the engine of their family vehicle. This requires an understanding of a somewhat idiomatic use of the verb "to run" but the context involving a motor vehicle brings clarity.

The pragmatic meaning—the thrust she desires the son to catch, understand, and apply (i.e., what the mother is *doing* with what she's saying)—is not as immediately apparent. On one hand, they could be words of reprimand as the mother is reminding her son, yet again, to turn off the car when he comes into the house so as to not waste fuel and unnecessarily pollute the environment. On the other hand, these words could just as likely be a declaration of success as the vehicle has returned from the mechanic and, while it was previously broken, it is now working again. Yet another option is that of an announcement of preparedness for departure tantamount to "We're ready to go." Finally, "The car is running" could be a statement of impatience—an attempt by the mother to hurry her son out the door as his father is waiting in the car to drive him to soccer practice. You see, until the pragmatic meaning of the utterance is properly determined, the semantic meaning will not be enough to allow the son to know what action to take so as to satisfy the maternal demand of the saying.

Kuruvilla suggests that, as in the example provided above, what the mother is *doing* is projecting an ideal world in which, perhaps, the car is never left running in the driveway or the son willingly chips in for the completed auto repairs.[57] Depending on the pragmatic meaning of the saying, the mother desires the son to live in this ideal world by hearing her words, identifying and understanding the thrust (i.e., intended purpose) of the message, and submitting to the demand of that ideal world through application. This is how the mother (i.e., author) does things with what she says.

Like the mother above, the biblical authors (and, *the* biblical Author) are *doing* things with what they say. There exists an intended purpose to each segment of the inspired text, the identification of which is crucial for the development of not only valid interpretation but valid application.[58] Without an understanding of the pragmatic meaning of the pericope, application of the text is a guessing game. Comprehension of a text's semantic meaning is simply insufficient.

If a preacher fails to discern, for example, why the author includes the thrice-repeated motivation of Jonah's flight from God (i.e., to get away "from the presence of the Lord") (1:3 [x2], 10) or the compassionate determination of the pagan sailors to avoid throwing Jonah overboard (1:13a) even though they knew he caused the danger, he deserved punishment, and his

---

57. Kuruvilla, "Pericopal Theology," 11–12.

58. Kuruvilla, "Pericopal Theology," 12.

death would save their lives (1:12, 14), this leaves the door open to any and all interpretations of that pericope and, thus, applications.[59] Likewise, if the son fails to rightly discern and understand the intended purpose of his mother's kitchen communique, he may end up celebrating the good work of the family mechanic rather than rushing out the door to appease his waiting father. In both cases, valid application is in jeopardy because the thrust of what has been communicated has not been properly understood, the desire of the A/author has not been rightly identified, and the ideal world has not been stepped into.

Likewise in preaching. Before valid application can be confidently suggested to a congregation, the intended thrust of the segment of Scripture being exposited (i.e., the pericope) must be recovered, showcased, and communicated. Once what Jonah is doing with what he is saying is discerned—once the theology of the pericope is identified—only then can modern, valid relevance be properly seen, understood, applied, and enjoyed.

Now, when we assume, as has already been discussed, that the biblical text is not an end in and of itself but rather a means to hearer transformation into the image and likeness of Jesus Christ, the preacher can assume that the inspired thrust of any given pericope of God's word, if submitted to and applied, will inevitably move a believer closer to God's ideal world, the world in which he desires and invites his people to live and to propagate. Thus, in the identification and communication of the thrust of a given pericope—what the author is doing with what he is saying—the expositor is really uncovering a segment of the ideal world—a sliver of the ideal—in which God is inviting his people to occupy should they submit to his divine demands therein.[60]

If the above statements are to be accepted as true, it then follows that if a preacher communicates consecutive segments of this divinely revealed ideal world week after week, pericope after pericope, book after book, and sermon after sermon, the cumulative effect will inevitably be that God's ideal world, a world revealed in its desired totality in the entirety of the canon, is progressively unveiled and, by the power of God's Spirit, applied and dwelled in by God's people.[61] Kuruvilla represents this process visually in a similar way as that which follows:[62]

59. For a treatment of this specific text, see appendix B.

60. For a more comprehensive description of the identification and role of divine demand, see Kuruvilla, *Privilege the Text!*, 151–209.

61. It is little wonder why, with this in mind, Kuruvilla strongly encourages preaching through books of the Bible rather than topical preaching. "[M]y strong recommendation is that you 'read continuously' (i.e., *lectio continua*), going from pericope to pericope in a given book, respecting the author's thought and the progression of his ideas." Kuruvilla, *Manual for Preaching*, 4.

62. Kuruvilla, "Pericopal Theology," 13.

PERICOPE	SEGMENT OF THE WORLD	CANONICAL WORLD
Pericope 1	Segment 1 of Canonical World	
Pericope 2	Segment 2 of Canonical World	
Pericope 3	Segment 3 of Canonical World	God's Ideal World
Pericope 4	Segment 4 of Canonical World	
…	…	
Pericope n	Segment n of Canonical World	

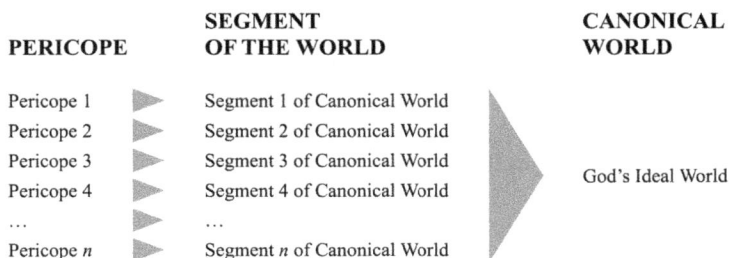

Figure 2.1. Pericopal Theology and God's Ideal World

With this approach in mind, "each sermon on a particular pericope is God's gracious invitation to mankind to live in his ideal world by abiding by the thrust of that pericope—i.e., the requirements of God's ideal world as called for in that pericope's world-segment."[63] Because the ideal world presented in the Bible is created by, sustained by, belonging to, and communicated by God, "theology" is an appropriate term and, thus

> the segment of this ideal world that each pericope projects becomes the theology of that pericope. To live by the theology of the pericope is to accept God's gracious invitation to inhabit his ideal world; by so doing, his people align themselves to the precepts, priorities, and practices of that ideal world—i.e., to the will of God . . . So, sermon by sermon, and pericope by pericope, more and more facets of life are aligned to divine will.[64]

What the utilization of pericopal theology proposes is a theological exegesis that gives the inspired text itself priority, essentially allowing it to speak for itself and reveal its own agenda. If the preacher assumes that the author is doing something with what he is saying, clues to the thrust of a writing are discoverable through a "directed exploration that searches specifically for those gold nuggets of pericopal theology."[65]

If, for example, a preacher suggests from Jonah 2 that "The prayers of God's people are to be consistent with the compassionate character of the God they are called to reflect to others," a hearer can look to the pericope in question and assess whether or not the thrust suggested from the

63. Kuruvilla, "Pericopal Theology," 13.

64. Kuruvilla, "Pericopal Theology," 14. For a description of how pericopal theology differs from biblical and systematic theology, see Kuruvilla, "Christiconic Interpretation," 132–34.

65. Kuruvilla, "Pericopal Theology," 15–16.

pulpit matches the evidence within the text itself. And if the same preacher, now handling the third chapter of the same book of the Bible, calls for his congregation to apply the text to their lives by "intentionally loving even 'outsiders' in their lives," the hearer can look to the text and ask, "Is this applicational fruit hanging solidly on the branches of the theology of the pericope stemming from the trunk of theological exegesis?"

EN ROUTE TO VALID APPLICATION: CHRISTICONIC HERMENEUTIC

With the text itself being given priority in determining its thrust, valid application can then be arrived at.[66] This application projects a segment of the plenary ideal world in which God is graciously inviting his people to dwell by, week after week, sermon after sermon, submitting to the requirements of this world outlined in each pericope. This theological approach "helps bring specific portions of the biblical text to bear upon the situation of the hearers, thereby aligning congregation to canon, God's people to God's Word."[67]

What about Christ? Paul seems to make it clear that Jesus should be quite involved in the sermonic process: "For I determined to know nothing among you except Jesus Christ, and Him crucified" (1 Cor 2:2). Tim Keller boldly states the case for christocentrism when he writes that "biblical accuracy and Christocentricity are the same thing to [the apostle] Paul. You can't properly preach any text—putting it into its rightful place in the whole Bible—unless you show how its themes find their fulfillment in the person of Christ."[68] Albert Mohler is another who represents this approach well: "Preach the Word, place it in its canonical context, and 'make a bee-line to the cross.'"[69] Preaching is to start with the Bible and end with Christ. Bryan Chapell adds his voice of support to the popular hermeneutic:

> The proper interpretation of any text requires regard for its context [which] includes not only its literary and historical setting but also its place in God's redemptive plan . . . all passages in their context serve our understanding of [Christ's] nature and/or necessity . . . Christ-centered preaching identifies the role of a text in the Bible's full testimony of God's gracious

66. Again, for application from a particular biblical pericope to be valid, it must be demonstrably built atop the divine demand of the text, that which is determined through right discernment of what the author is *doing* with what he is *saying*.

67. Kuruvilla, "Christiconic Interpretation," 134.

68. Keller, *Preaching*, 2. Emphasis added.

69. Mohler, *He Is Not Silent*, 21.

character, instruction, and actions, which are ultimately mani-
fested in Christ.[70]

According to this christocentric approach to Bible interpretation, Jesus
is present in all of Scripture and it is the expositor's job to find him—or even
sense him—and show him to the congregation. Certainly, it is true that the
incarnation of Jesus Christ illuminates much of the Old Testament. The tab-
ernacle, the law, the sacrificial system, the Jewish calendar, and the Egyptian
exodus all look different because of the "unignorable light" of Jesus. This is
part of the wonder of progressive revelation and what Jesus proved on the
road to Emmaus (Luke 24:27).[71]

However, this christocentric hermeneutical approach seems to allow
for and even, at times, demand speculation, innovation, and imagination
from biblical interpreters. "But it is hard to defend a stance that locates
Christ in every word, verse, and story without the interpreter engaging in
some hermeneutical acrobatics."[72] Kuruvilla proposes a christiconic hermeneutical approach that discerns an implicit picture of Christ in each segment of Scripture, while a christocentric interpretation demands Christ be
found explicitly in each pericope.[73]

As has already been described, God has graciously invited his people to
live in an ideal world—a world governed by his precepts, priorities, and practices.[74] To do that, however, God's people must submit to the requirements of
that world, divine demands that are found in each pericope of Scripture. By
submitting to those divine demands and applying them to the life of individual believers, pericope by pericope, the people of God are increasingly and
progressively made to inhabit God's ideal, plenary, canonical world. There
has been only one man in the history of the world that has perfectly met all
of God's requirements and therefore successfully, comprehensively, and thor-
oughly dwelt in the ideal world the Father presents in Scripture—the Lord

70. Gibson and Kim, *Homiletics and Hermeneutics*, 3–16.

71. "The two Testaments look to Jesus Christ, the Old as its expectation and the New
as its model, and both have him as their center." Pascal, *Pensees and Other Writings*, 5.

72. Kuruvilla, "Christiconic Interpretation," 135. For detailed and thorough argu-
ments against a christocentric hermeneutic, see Kuruvilla, *Privilege the Text!*, 238–69;
or Chou, "Hermeneutical Evaluation."

73. Kuruvilla, *Vision for Preaching*, 138–39.

74. "This canonical world projected by Scripture depicts a mode of existence in
which God's precepts operate, his priorities are supreme, and his practices are enacted:
'precepts'—why things happen in the *world in front of the text*; 'priorities'—what things
matter in *the world in front of the text*; and 'practices'—how things run in the *world in
front of the text*. This, God's ideal world, is where his precepts are acted upon, his priorities are upheld, and his practices are conformed to." Kuruvilla, *Privilege the Text!*, 100.

Jesus Christ (2 Cor 5:21; Heb 4:15; 7:26).[75] While members of a congregation will imperfectly stumble their way toward God's ideal, Jesus accomplished it perfectly. "Jesus Christ alone has comprehensively abided by the theology of every pericope of Scripture. In other words, each pericope of the Bible is actually portraying a characteristic of Christ, showing us what it means to perfectly fulfill, as he did, the particular call of that pericope."[76]

Consider, for example, Proverbs 25:16: "Have you found honey? Eat only what you need, that you not have it in excess and vomit it." A christo-centric hermeneutic presupposes that this proverbial statement "is directly and explicitly related to the Second Person of the Trinity."[77] This method of interpretation demands that the above verse must point toward, fore-shadow, anticipate, or witness to the promise of salvation now accomplished in Christ.[78] How could that be? Is Jesus the honey to be sought, found, and devoured (by faith) in moderation? Perhaps the sin of gluttony is merely being warned against, a sin that Christ paid for on the cross. If that is the case, then application would simply be something like, "Thank God for his forgiveness of overconsumption." However the passage is explained and applied using a christocentric hermeneutic, it is difficult to justify Christ's direct and explicit involvement therein.

Alternatively, a christiconic interpretation allows the text to make the ethical demand it clearly makes—that of the avoidance of gluttonous activ-ity. How? Because no other human aside from the Lord Jesus Christ has perfectly lived a gluttony-free life.[79] Thus, if a believer recognizes the divine demand of the text and applies it to their life by the power of the Holy Spirit (i.e., by avoiding over-consumption and instead using only what is needed), not only do they side-step physical consequences (e.g., vomiting), but they also take one step toward Christlikeness.

The implications of the implementation of a christiconic interpreta-tion in preaching can be seen visually in what follows:[80]

---

75. Kuruvilla, *Vision for Preaching*, 143.

76. Kuruvilla, *Vision for Preaching*, 143–44.

77. Kuruvilla, *Privilege the Text!*, 239.

78. A christocentric hermeneutic is sometimes referred to as a "redemptive-histori-cal hermeneutic" and sees every pericope of Scripture through the lens of the whole. In other words, the whole canon is used to (re)interpret the parts.

79. That Jesus Christ was never guilty of gluttony is known not because it is explic-itly stated in the Gospel accounts, but because he was the perfect man (2 Cor 5:21; Heb 4:15; 1 Pet 2:22; 1 John 3:5).

80. Kuruvilla, *Vision for Preaching*, 144.

PERICOPE	THEOLOGY: FACET OF IMAGE	CANON: PLENARY IMAGE
Pericope 1	Facet 1 of Image of Christ	
Pericope 2	Facet 2 of Image of Christ	
Pericope 3	Facet 3 of Image of Christ	
Pericope 4	Facet 4 of Image of Christ	Canonical Image of Christ
...	...	
Pericope *n*	Facet *n* of Image of Christ	

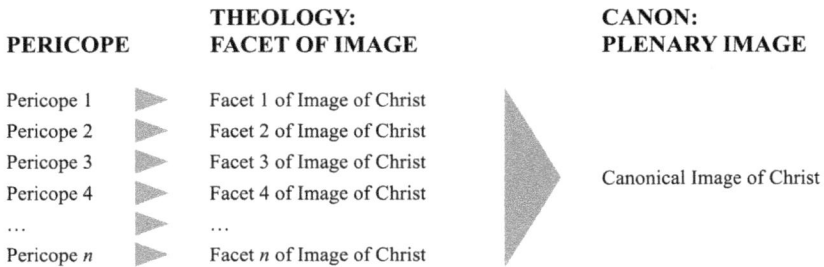

Figure 2.2. Christiconic Hermeneutic and the Canonical Image of Christ

God's ultimate goal for his people is to be conformed to the image of his incarnate Son (Rom 8:29; 2 Cor 3:18; Eph 3:19; Col 1:28). Preaching facilitates this conformation by the power of the Holy Spirit working through the Scriptures as, week after week, pericope after pericope, sermon after sermon, facets of Christ's character are identified and God's people align themselves to his image.

CONCLUSION

A vital facet of the corporate worship of God's people is God's word most powerfully exemplified in its preaching. A vital element of biblical preaching is the development and communication of valid application as Scripture itself claims that its application is crucial. It is the task of the preacher to guide God's people from the *then* to the *now*.

Unfortunately, to date little has been written regarding the process by which any preacher can make this move and develop valid applications for his people. Many suggestions have been proposed on how best to bridge this chasm of space between an ancient text and a modern people. The goal is faithful, biblical, text-driven exegesis that allows for valid, comprehendible, and relevant application.

Abraham Kuruvilla's pericopal theology and christiconic hermeneutic comprise an interpretive approach that may address some of the concerns that exist in previous methodologies (e.g., christocentric interpretation) and attempts to remove the seemingly subjective components of moving from text to praxis. By privileging the text and sitting under preaching that utilizes a theological hermeneutic, God's people will not only be able to better understand what God is saying semantically, but will be able to discern what

God is doing pragmatically with what he's saying. When these two realities are understood and seen in the inspired text itself, valid application can be heard with confidence and applied with conviction.

3

Organization of the Study

THIS RESEARCH PROJECT WAS undertaken with the ultimate goal of exploring and evaluating the implementation and effectiveness of pericopal theology and a christiconic hermeneutic in the homiletical process. Particular attention was given to the development and communication of valid application of specific biblical pericopes characterized by clear and observable fidelity to the Scriptures and biblically supportable modern-day relevance for hearers. To this end, linguistic, exegetical, and theological work was done in the book of Jonah, a corresponding four-week expository sermon series was preached, and a self-administered pretest and posttest survey was distributed that focused on the theology of Jonah's four pericopes and their practical implications for God's people today. Participants in the study (i.e., those who heard and/or viewed all four sermons and completed the survey both beforehand and afterward) were largely members of Oakridge Bible Chapel (OBC) in Oakville, Ontario, Canada.[1] The data collected via the bookended surveys was then analyzed against the three hypotheses, validating the hypotheses or refining them to accurately reflect the trends revealed therein. This chapter describes the process of survey development and evaluation in more detail.

---

1. As will be described below, some participants were outside of the OBC church family and participated through online mediums (e.g., podcast, online service streaming, and prerecorded video sermons). The data collection portion of this project took place in the midst of the 2020–2021 coronavirus outbreak and, thus, electronic consumption of and participation in church-related ministries was higher and more common than in years prior.

RESEARCH QUESTION AND HYPOTHESES

In academic study, the research question "is a way of explaining as sharply and as pithily as possible to yourself exactly what you are going to research and what you wish to find out . . . [and] must therefore be framed in a positive manner, be value-neutral, and be capable of being proven right or wrong on the basis of empirical evidence."[2] Said otherwise, the research question is developed for the researcher as an attempt to encapsulate the motivation for the study in a handleable statement that allows for and anticipates discovery.

With the above definition and explanation in mind, the research question specifically being addressed in the current project was as follows: Can the utilization of pericopal theology and the implementation of a christiconic hermeneutic aid in a preacher's identification and communication of valid application and the hearer's comprehension of that application? In other words, does the specific method of interpretation in question have an observable effect on both the preacher and the hearer of the sermon and, more specifically, does it help in the development, transmission, and understanding of biblically warranted practical application? With this question fueling the current project, three hypotheses were proposed, provided structure to the research, and were followed.

Hypothesis 1: Growth in Biblical Knowledge

The first hypothesis of the current project is that through the utilization of pericopal theology and a christiconic hermeneutic and the subsequent preaching of an expository sermon series there will be measurable growth in congregational knowledge of the biblical text.

John Calvin once wrote that "If true religion is to beam upon us, our principle must be, that it is necessary to begin with heavenly teaching, and that it is impossible for any man to obtain even the minutest portion of right and sound doctrine without being a disciple of Scripture."[3] Kent Hughes, similarly but more simply, has asserted that "The better informed we are [as Christians], the better we can worship."[4] The principle is this: The more God's people understand the God they serve as he has revealed himself in his written word, the better they are able to live lives that honor him, reflect his character, and carry out his will (Rom 12:1–2).

2. Birley and Moreland, *Practical Guide to Academic Research*, 7, 9.

3. Calvin, *Institutes of the Christian Religion*, 1.6.2.

4. Hughes, *Disciplines of a Godly Man*, 114.

To allow for the transforming of minds, God's people would do well to better know what it is the Bible says, what was going on at the time of the original writing, what argument(s) the author was making, what it is the author was trying to communicate through the words he uses, and what effect the author intended the writing would have or what action he wanted his audience to take. It was expected that a four-week expository sermon series would stimulate such growth in hearers and that, after sitting under text-driven, text-centered teaching, God's people would, at the very least, better know the text of Jonah.[5]

Hypothesis 2: Growth in Theological Understanding

The second hypothesis of the current project is that through the utilization of pericopal theology and a christiconic hermeneutic and the subsequent preaching of an expository sermon series a measurable growth in congregational understanding of the *theology* of the biblical text—both as a whole and as individual pericopes—will be observed.

In Bible interpretation, such as what happens in the act of sermon preparation, there exists the original context of the biblical writing, the current context of the modern hearer, and a chasm of time, space, language, and culture between the two that must be traversed in order to develop valid application. Theology, rooted firmly in the *then* of the inspired text, can serve to bridge that gap and be the apparatus on which modern Christians can hang relevant application.

This project will explore the idea that, while biblical and systematic theology certainly have indispensable value in the homiletical process (serving as guardrails for the interpretive process, ensuring study does not veer off the edge of orthodoxy), it is *pericopal* theology that allows for unique, varied, and valid application to be developed.[6] It is expected that, following a four-week expository sermon series in which the preacher demonstrates

---

5. It would be hypothesized that *any* sermon series tethered to a particular biblical text—utilizing pericopal theology, christiconic hermeneutics, or otherwise—would produce an increase in hearer knowledge of the Scripture(s) being preached. Thus, this first hypothesis is not unique to the method being studied in this work. However, it was understood as a necessary foundational category atop which the following two hypotheses were built, both of which grow in specificity to pericopal theology and a christiconic hermeneutic.

6. Kuruvilla, *Ephesians*, 2. Here, the author defines the theology of the pericope as "the ideological vehicle through which divine precepts, priorities, and practices are propounded for appropriation by readers."

the pericopal theology of each passage of Scripture, the hearers will show a marked growth in their understanding of the theology of each pericope.

Hypothesis 3: Growth in Applicational Discernment

The third and final hypothesis of the current project is that through the utilization of pericopal theology and a christiconic hermeneutic and the subsequent preaching of an expository sermon series a measurable growth in congregational discernment of the divine demand placed on God's people through the biblical text (i.e., the application) will be observable.

Once the preacher has led hearers from the biblical text to the theology of the pericope, a move to praxis *must* follow. Kuruvilla has noted that "Only in personal application does the text accomplish its meaning."[7] Not only does the preacher desire that hearers know the biblical text and understand the theology underpinning its timelessness, but he also desires their discernment of *how* and *why* the thrust of a text is simultaneously a divine invitation to God's people to live lives increasingly aligned to the values of God's kingdom (i.e., Christlikeness). This project will explore the idea that a christiconic hermeneutic most faithfully and consistently accomplishes this agenda and that by the end of a four-week sermon series hearers will demonstrate a growth in their ability to identify the divine demand placed upon them from each pericope of Scripture.

RESEARCH METHOD AND PROCEDURES: AN OVERVIEW

With the above research question and hypotheses in place, the next step of the current project was the identification and selection of a method of research that would be most appropriate to the stated goals. Thus, a program development and evaluation was selected. As, at the time of this writing, a limited amount of work has been done on the use and evaluation of pericopal theology and a christiconic hermeneutic, a program had to be created for the purposes of the study. In addition, since the program to be evaluated was a series of expository sermons on the book of Jonah—something certainly and necessarily uniquely taught by any given preacher—the program would have to be likewise unique and tailored to the specific messages preached.

---

7. Kuruvilla, *Privilege the Text!*, 136.

To this end, the translation, exegesis, and theological work was done in the biblical text of Jonah following the example of Abraham Kuruvilla in his works on Genesis, Judges, Mark, Ephesians, 1 and 2 Timothy, and Titus,[8] a process he describes and summarizes as a

> *theological* exegesis that privileges the text, looking for clues to its theology—not a random dig but a directed one that searches specifically for those gold nuggets of pericopal theology. Within every text, there are literary and stylistic traces of authors' agendas, evidence pointing to the authors' *doings*, signs that lead to the discovery of pericopal theology. But only a privileging of the text by theological exegesis will discover that precious ore.[9]

The theological exegesis of the book of Jonah resulted in the articulation of the theology of each of the four pericopes, the thrusts of each text, and the divine demands intended by the author.[10] These, like a scientific hypothesis, were then tested repeatedly against the biblical text, changing, shifting, and crafting each until sufficient correspondence and representation of the pericopes was achieved.

Once the above work was finished and the thrusts and divine demands were tested against the biblical text to ensure fidelity, only then could valid application be sought and stated with conviction, and sermon maps and manuscripts crafted.[11] This process of moving from a biblical book to pericopal theology to thrust identification and articulation to sermon mapping to sermon manuscript followed the example, again, of Kuruvilla.[12]

It was necessary for the exegetical, theological, and homiletical work to be completed prior to the development of the pretest and posttest tool that would eventually be used to evaluate the congregation's growing biblical, theological, and applicational understandings. Once pericopal theologies, thrusts, and divine demands were satisfactorily in place, these were used as guides to create a survey that was comprehensive, challenging, and robust enough to provide adequate data for the researcher while, at the same time,

---

8. See Kuruvilla, *Mark*; *Genesis*; *Ephesians*; *Judges*; and *1–2 Timothy, Titus*.

9. Kuruvilla, *Vision for Preaching*, 103.

10. For a summary of this textual work, see appendix A. It should be noted that the theological thrust of each pericope is in no way an attempt to distill the passage in question into a bite-sized statement that functionally replaces the inspired text. Indeed, nothing can accomplish that goal without loss. Rather, the articulation of a theological thrust or theological focus is for the preacher alone, that he may arrange the different movements of the text so as to best communicate the whole to the intended hearers and hit them with the full intended force of that pericope.

11. For sermon maps and manuscripts of all four pericopes of Jonah, see appendix B.

12. See Kuruvilla, *Manual for Preaching*.

being user-friendly, accessible, and understandable enough to not discourage participation. This tool had to measure the participant's understanding of both what the biblical author is *saying* as well as what he is *doing* with what he is saying. Only with an understanding of both can hearers then rightly discern appropriate application for their lives.

RESEARCH PARTICIPANTS

The research participants for this project were chiefly members of Oakridge Bible Chapel (OBC) in Oakville, Ontario, Canada, the local church congregation that the researcher currently serves as primary teaching pastor. In addition to attendees of OBC, there were a limited number of members of other church families involved, and the developed evaluation tool requested the participants to disclose whether they are a member of "Oakridge" or "other." The only requirement for participation in the current study was a willingness to complete the survey two times, one on each side of attending, listening to, or viewing all four sermons on the Old Testament book of Jonah. There was no obligation for participation and the decision to do so was done in anonymity as individuals were invited to pick up surveys from the church.

Provided below is a demographic breakdown of the participants in the current project based upon information volunteered in the evaluation tool. As can be seen, those participating in the study varied in gender, age, years of experience as a Christian, and level of formal Bible training. The vast majority of participants self-reported regular church attendance and most identified OBC as their home church, a congregation that, on Sunday morning, ranges in attendance from about 180 to 250.

Table 3.1. Project Participants: Survey Completion Percentage by Gender				
	Male	Female	Undisclosed	Total No.
Completed Pretest Survey	33	46	2	81
Completed Posttest Survey	25	38	2	65
Percentage Completed (%)	75.8	82.6	100.0	80.3

Table 3.2. Project Participants: Age							
	12–17	25–34	35–44	45–54	55–64	65–74	75+
Number	2	6	4	12	18	10	13
% of Total	3.1	9.2	6.2	18.5	27.7	15.4	20.0

Table 3.3. Project Participants: Years as a Christian				
	5–9	10–14	15–19	20+
Number	2	3	5	55
% of Total	3.1	7.7	4.6	84.6

Table 3.4. Project Participants: Formal Bible Training						
	None	Camp	Some Bible College	Bible College Degree	Some Seminary	Seminary Degree
Number	40	8	5	3	3	6
% of Total	61.5	12.3	7.7	4.6	4.6	9.2

Table 3.5. Project Participants: Church Attendance					
	1–4 Times Per Year	About Once a Month	About Every Other Week	About Every Sunday	No Response
Number	0	0	1	63	1
% of Total	0	0	1.5	96.9	1.5

Table 3.6. Project Participants: Church Membership		
	Oakridge Bible Chapel	Other
Number	57	8
% of Total	87.7	12.3

RESEARCH INSTRUMENT

The instrument of evaluation used for this current project was a self-administered pretest and posttest survey. The rationale for the chosen testing method is well articulated by Floyd Fowler Jr.: "The purpose of the survey is to produce statistics, that is, quantitative or numerical descriptions about some aspects of the study population . . . [and the] main way of collecting information is by asking people questions; their answers constitute the data to be analyzed."[13] Given the stated hypotheses driving the current study, this was determined to be the best method for evaluation.

13. Fowler, *Survey Research Methods*, 1.

The use of a quantitative pretest and posttest instrument provided an observable and numeric description of the degree of growth achieved in each participant as well as the degree of growth achieved across the total population of participants. Being able to see trends of growth at both the micro and macro levels added robustness to the study and highlighted potential outliers. Employing the use of the same survey for both the pretest and posttest instrument allowed for a reliable means of assessing how the use of pericopal theology and a christiconic hermeneutic affected the hearers' understanding of both the biblical author's *sayings* (i.e., growing in biblical understanding) and the author's *doings* (i.e., growing in theological and applicational understanding of the book of Jonah).

The pretest and posttest survey was designed to be anonymous and self-administered, allowing and encouraging participants to respond honestly and without fear of exposure or public failure and, thus, serving as a reliable indicator of their actual responses to the questions regarding their understanding of the contents of the book of Jonah as well as the pericopal theology and divine demand of each pericope. Pressure to respond in a particular way was attenuated by not having an interviewer or the researcher personally conduct the survey with the participant and by ensuring their anonymity. This survey can be viewed in appendix C.

Instrument Development and Description

As the hypotheses for the current research were threefold, the instrument to be used had to be designed to catch data that regards all three questions. Thus, in its design, care was taken to do just that.

As has already been stated, the exegetical and theological work in the text had to be accomplished prior to the creation of the instrument to ensure that what was communicated through the four-week expository sermon series was consistent with the questions and desired responses on the survey both before and after the series. Because of this, once the exegetical and theological study was completed and the thrusts of each pericope (i.e., the theological foci) were articulated and tested,[14] divine demands were identified, valid applications were suggested, and sermon maps were established.

Once the necessary information was established from the biblical text of Jonah, the survey was developed. The goals for developing the survey were as follows: (1) The tool would be comprehensive in dealing with the whole of the biblical text. (2) The tool would cover both the author's *doings*

---

14. A note of appreciation must be added to Abraham Kuruvilla for his oversight, input, and approval of the final theological foci used for the sermon series and study.

and *sayings*. (3) The tool would evaluate the participant's understanding of the divine demand of each pericope. (4) The tool would avoid being overwhelming, cumbersome, and overly complicated. (5) The tool would be short enough so as to encourage completion both before and after the sermon series. (6) The tool itself would be educational for participants, encouraging and guiding them to consider what the biblical text—and the God who inspired the text—is *actually* saying and calling for them to do in response. With all of these goals in place, much care and effort was expended on the development of the survey.

In an effort to make the tool as short as possible without sacrificing any of the complementary goals, it was decided to use a twenty-five-question survey. These twenty-five questions were divided up between the four pericopes of Jonah with six questions designated to each and a final question concerning the book as a whole unit. Of the six questions for each pericope, the first three explored the author's *sayings* (i.e., details about the text) (Hypothesis 1). Following these three questions came a question regarding the *thrust*[15] of the passage (Hypothesis 2) and, finally, two questions regarding the *divine demand*[16] placed upon the people of God by the word of God and an appropriate *applicational command*[17] rooted therein (Hypothesis 3). The tool was designed to lead the participant through the process of text to application for each pericope of Scripture, mirroring in the survey what was done in the pulpit by the preacher. This means moving from observing the *sayings* of the author (three questions) to identifying the *thrust* of the text (i.e., the theology of the pericope) (one question) and, finally, to the understanding of the *divine demand* such a thrust places upon the people of God (one question) and how that naturally works itself out in their lives today (i.e., the *applicational command*) (one question). The structure of the research instrument is visually represented in the table below.

---

15. The explanation of this term is given on the instrument itself: "The *thrust* of a text refers to what the author is *doing* with what he is *saying*. He is using words to accomplish something, and the *thrust* is an attempt to succinctly articulate what that is!"

16. The explanation is provided on the instrument itself: "The *divine demand* is the specific call of God in a specific passage of Scripture for his people to live a specific way for their good and his glory."

17. The explanation is provided on the instrument itself: "Rooted in a right understanding of a passage's *thrust* and *divine demand*, an *applicational command* is an authoritative assignment from God to his people."

No.	PERICOPE 1	PERICOPE 2	PERICOPE 3	PERICOPE 4	WHOLE BOOK
			Table 3.7. Research Instrument Structure		
1	Sayings				
2	Sayings				
3	Sayings				
4	Thrust				
5	Div. Demand				
6	App. Command				
7		Sayings			
8		Sayings			
9		Sayings			
10		Thrust			
11		Div. Demand			
12		App. Command			
13			Sayings		
14			Sayings		
15			Sayings		
16			Thrust		
17			Div. Demand		
18			App. Command		
19				Sayings	
20				Sayings	
21				Sayings	
22				Thrust	
23				Div. Demand	
24				App. Command	
25					Thrust

The questions regarding the authorial *sayings*, while somewhat arbitrary,[18] were crafted to be both relatively difficult and obviously textual. This dual purpose was important as the intention was to measure growth

18. By this is meant that of all the many details of a given pericope, three had to be selected.

in participant's understanding of the contents of the book of Jonah and not their knowledge of details so obscure that they would never have found them without the help of the preacher. For example, a question as obvious as "What was the prophet swallowed by?" would be of little use for measuring growth as most people would know the answer to that question regardless of whether or not they had ever actually read the book of Jonah. On the other end of the spectrum was the avoidance of questions so difficult that a seminary degree, knowledge of biblical Hebrew, or familiarity with advanced literary theory would be necessary to answer. Ultimately, the goal was to have the questions regarding authorial *sayings* reflect and teach the importance of paying close attention to the text itself, identifying details that are important to the articulation of the authorial thrust.

The questions regarding the biblical text, pericopal theology, and application were all crafted with the developed sermon maps in mind. While not necessarily communicating each verbatim, the general idea was that participant's (growing) understanding of authorial intent, pericopal theology, and divine demand could be seen as resulting from increased familiarity with the biblical text rather than memorized from the pastor's notes. Table 3.7 provides a visual overview of the tool, what each question (column 1) sought to explore, and how each question added to the whole.[19]

To aid in the usability of the tool as well as the ease and objectivity of the data collection and analysis portion of the study, multiple-choice questions were utilized. For each of the twenty-five questions, participants were asked to choose the best or most appropriate from six possible answers. The five incorrect responses were developed from potential popular culture misunderstandings of the passage and suggestions made by other authors and preachers of the book of Jonah that this researcher felt misidentified and miscommunicated the thrust of the passage and, thus, provided negative examples of Bible interpretation and application. Some examples of this will follow.

Question 2 of the survey asked: "What was Jonah's stated motivation for disobeying God in chapter 1?" The following potential answers were provided from which participants were asked to choose: "(a) Fleeing God's assignment, (b) Fleeing God's presence, (c) Fleeing wickedness, (d) Fleeing God's judgement, (e) The chapter doesn't tell us, and (f) I'm not sure."

While the first four options all seem plausible and include the idea of fleeing, a detail most Christians, if they know anything about the story of Jonah at all, can recall, the question implies that the text gives a specific

19. This is a reminder that the thrust and divine demand are expressions and component parts of the author's doings. The applicational command is an expression of the valid application rooted in the pericopal theology of the text.

rationale and motivation for the prophetic retreat. Indeed, thrice the text informs readers that it was "from the presence of the Lord" that Jonah intended and strove to run, not an unimportant detail when seeking to understand the thrust of this opening pericope. Thus, this question regarding the author's *sayings* in Jonah 1 highlights the importance of paying attention to the text itself and avoiding the importing of assumed motivations unto the prophet.

Question 22 posits: "What best describes the main point, *thrust*, or focus that God is communicating through the text of Jonah 4? (Note: While all the below statements may be biblical, not all are the primary teaching of this particular chapter of Scripture.)" The provided options for responding were as follows: "(a) As an extension of his character, God shows mercy to whom he will show mercy, offering salvation to even the most vile sinner; (b) God's people are to reflect God's compassion to others by understanding and submitting to his will at the expense of their own; (c) For God's people, anger and frustration with God and his ways reveals the idolatry, prejudice, and sinfulness in our hearts; (d) Like Jesus, God's people are to confront prejudices in our world; unlike Jesus, sometimes they exist within our own hearts; and (e) God's sovereignty in salvation (that he wisely and powerfully decides to whom He will extend compassion and mercy) is true regardless of how his people understand and accept that reality."

Once again, many of these potential answers are plausible, yet, as this researcher argues, one is far more defensible from the actual text of Jonah 4 than the others. Many of the potential answers provided intentionally included characteristics common in much homiletic thought and practice today (e.g., christocentrism) (option [d] above), a hermeneutic that privileges (1) the New Testament text as a means of understanding rightly the Old Testament text, (2) biblical theology, (3) systematic theology, or (4) the emphasis on salvation from all passages (option [a] above). While many of the potential answers are supportable using *biblical* theology,[20] only one is supportable using *pericopal* theology, and thus, only one can lead to the appropriate identification of the divine demand and valid application.

The tool used for this study went through many revisions prior to distribution. The tool was also sent to fifteen individuals for a "test drive" (i.e., for feedback on its usefulness, accessibility, clarity, and suggested length of

---

20. For example, is it true that "For God's people, anger and frustration with God and His ways reveals the idolatry, prejudice, and sinfulness in our hearts"? Few would say "no," and many passages of Scripture can be used to support this idea. The question becomes, however: Is this the thrust of Jonah 4? If not, then to mistakenly identify it as such would be to, first, misspeak for God, and, second, fail to communicate what God *actually* is saying through this passage.

time it would take future participants to complete the survey). Below is the note used to solicit final feedback from volunteers for the purpose of final revisions prior to the distribution of the pretest.

> As you know, I'm in the (hopefully!) final stages of some school- ing and, as part of that process, I'm required to complete a research project. I'm primarily using my church family as the test subjects and have developed a tool (attached) that they will complete before and after a sermon series on the book of Jonah measuring their growing understanding of the biblical text as well as its call for application on their lives.
>
> Before I go "live" with it, however, I'd like to get rid of as many stumbling blocks within the survey as I can. *That's where I'm asking for your help.* If you'd be willing, I'd appreciate you reading through this draft of the survey (you don't have to actu- ally *do* it) and letting me know if there's anything unclear, con- fusing, or anything else that hinders its completion.

The feedback received from these individuals proved helpful in smoothing out some of the language used and polishing the user-friendly nature of the instrument. Of particular interest were the footnoted explana- tions of *thrust, divine demand,* and *applicational command,* terms almost certainly novel to the participants and, yet, important to use for the sake of the study. Once the necessary changes were made, the main advisor of the current research was consulted a final time, and the instrument was printed and prepared for distribution.

Research Procedures and Collection of Data

Once the research instrument reached its final form, notification and expla- nation needed to be provided to the congregation and potential participants in order to garner interest, encourage involvement, and solicit help in the project. To this end, informal announcements and brief explanations were given from the OBC pulpit before and after corporate worship a number of weeks prior to the formal start of the study and Jonah sermon series. The intention of these announcements was largely to raise awareness and stoke anticipation for both the upcoming sermon series and the study. Knowing that weekly Sunday morning attendance is not always consistent, this was repeated several weeks in a row in an effort to communicate with as many Oakridge attendees as possible.

As the time drew nearer for the scheduled sermon series on the book of Jonah to begin, three weeks were allotted for participants to pick up, complete, and submit their pretest surveys, and a formal announcement of the study with full explanation of its demands on participants took place. To accomplish this, a video recording was distributed to the church family along with its transcript via email. It was also posted on the church website, and many congregants asked permission to share the invitation with Christian friends and family that attended other assemblies. The email and website post included links to the pretest survey, instructions as to how to complete the tool, and options for how to submit it when finished. Below is the transcript of that invitation to take part.

Greetings, all!

As some of you already know, I am nearing what I hope is the finish line of some schooling I've been working on over the past few years. One of the requirements of the program I'm in is a final research project and, to finish it, I need you. So, consider this the posting of a "help wanted" sign.

Let me begin by explaining what it is I'm studying and then I'll explain what it is I'm asking you do to help.

What I'm Doing

The apostle James makes it clear that, as Christians, we are to be doers of the word of God and not merely hearers of it (1:22–25; see also Matt 7:24–27; Rom 2:13). In other words, we're supposed to allow the Bible to change our lives and not simply collect information about it.

And one of the primary jobs of a pastor—one who, week after week, preaches God's word to God's people—is to not only properly explain the Bible but to help people apply the Bible to their lives.

My research, in a nutshell, is studying how a series of sermons on a particular book of the Bible affects the ability of a congregation to do two related but distinct things: first, help people understand what God is saying in that book and, second, help people understand what God wants us to do with what he's saying in that book. To put it in question form: Can preaching help God's people be both hearers and doers of God's word? I'm looking at the effectiveness of a specific method of Bible interpretation to those ends, and I'm using the book of Jonah as a case study.

So, that's what I'm doing. Now, here's what I'm asking you to do to help me.

How You Can Help

I've developed a twenty-five-question survey [link embedded] on the book of Jonah. About half the questions have to do with what God is saying in the book—details about the story, characters, and events. The other half have more to do with the application of what God is saying; what God wants us to do in response to the book.

If you're willing, I'm going to ask that you complete this survey twice (once before and once after the four-week sermon series on Jonah) so I can track possible growth in the areas mentioned above. Plan to take about fifteen minutes to complete it each time. The results are anonymous, so you don't have to worry about how well you do or anything like that. I'm just asking for your participation.

The plan is to start the Jonah series on Sunday, September 13, and so I'll ask that you finish and submit the first survey before that morning. If you can't physically be with us at Oakridge, that's fine—listening to the sermon via podcast or watching it online works as well. The only other requirements for helping me in this project is that you hear all four sermons before completing and submitting the survey for a second time.

So, again: I'm asking for your help.

STEP 1: Get the survey (download here [link embedded] and print it out or pick up a hard copy from the church).
STEP 2: Complete and submit the survey before September 13. You can email your completed survey to [church email address] (to maintain anonymity) or drop it off physically at the church (see survey for options).
STEP 3: Attend, watch, or listen to all four sermons on Jonah.
STEP 4: Get the survey again.
STEP 5: Complete and submit it again. Easy!

If you have any questions about the research, the survey, or the process, please don't hesitate to reach out and ask. I'd love to offer a more detailed explanation than can be given here.

Thanks for considering helping—I truly appreciate it!

For the next number of weeks after the formal invitation was distributed, surveys were placed at the back of the church auditorium and in the foyer with appropriate signage so that those exiting after morning service or visiting the church building during the week could pick up a blank instrument to be completed and returned. Reminders were given from the pulpit each week and via email. Completed surveys were accepted until the moment the first sermon in the Jonah series began, after which data collection for the pretest surveys was concluded and no more submissions were accepted.

The sermon series on the book of Jonah lasted four weeks, during which time there was no data collection to be done. However, it was during this time that the data collected from the pretest surveys were entered into a spreadsheet created for this project, recording the demographic information volunteered by participants as well as their responses to each of the twenty-five questions and the percentages of correct answers in the categories of authorial *sayings*, *doings*, and total score.

On the final Sunday morning of the Jonah sermon series, blank posttest surveys were placed at the back of the auditorium again and another invitation to participate was announced from the pulpit to those who had completed the pretest survey. This was continued for three weeks with participants submitting their completed posttest surveys in a variety of ways as outlined on the tool itself. As the posttest surveys were returned, their provided identification codes were matched with those provided on their pretest surveys, entered into the same spreadsheet used to record the data from the first round of submissions alongside their initial submission, and the results of the two surveys were compared. Table 3.8 shows a visual representation of the order of events for the data collection and research schedule.

Table 3.8. Data Collection and Research Schedule	
Week No.	**Activities Undertaken**
1	Informal announcement and brief explanation to potential participants
2	Informal announcement and brief explanation to potential participants
3	Formal announcement and full explanation distributed to potential participants; Pretest made available for pickup
4	Pretest made available for pickup; Completed pretests collected
5	Pretest made available for pickup; Completed pretests collected
6	Pretest made available for pickup; Completed pretests collected
7	Final completed pretests collected; Sermon series begins (pericope 1)
8	Sermon series continues (pericope 2)
9	Sermon series continues (pericope 3)
10	Sermon series continues (pericope 4); Posttest made available for pick-up
11	Posttest made available for pickup; Completed posttests collected
12	Posttest made available for pickup; Completed posttests collected
13	Posttest made available for pickup; Completed posttests collected
14	Research concluded

CONCLUSION

This research project was designed to answer the research question: Can the implementation of pericopal theology and a christiconic hermeneutic aid in a preacher's identification and communication of valid application and the hearer's comprehension of that application? The research method selected was a program development and evaluation using a pretest and posttest instrument for data collection. The development of this instrument was informed by three hypotheses and shaped by the exegetical and theological work done in the book of Jonah. The participants of the study were volunteers and remained anonymous but came largely from the congregation of OBC, while others participated from around the world via online mediums.

4

Explanation of the Results

FOLLOWING THE COMPLETION OF the four-week series of expository sermons on the book of Jonah as well as the distribution, completion, and collection of both pretest and posttest surveys, the data gathered was recorded and analyzed. The research question being explored in this project was: Can the implementation of pericopal theology and a christiconic hermeneutic aid in a preacher's identification and communication of valid application and the hearer's comprehension of that application? This chapter presents the results yielded by this study.

Three hypotheses were posited and tested in this applied research project, each building upon the previous to culminate in the particular examination of the methodology being studied (i.e., pericopal theology and a christiconic hermeneutic) and its effect on the identification of valid application from the biblical text of Jonah. But, as has been discussed in this work already, to discern valid application the theology of the pericope must first be rightly understood, and to understand the theology of the pericope, what the author is *doing* with what he is *saying* must first be rightly identified. This progression can be noted in the three hypotheses listed below:

1. Through the utilization of pericopal theology, a christiconic hermeneutic, and the subsequent preaching of an expository sermon series, there will be measurable growth in congregational knowledge of the biblical text.

2. Through the utilization of pericopal theology, a christiconic hermeneutic, and the subsequent preaching of an expository sermon series, a measurable growth in congregational understanding of the *theology* of the biblical text—both as a whole and as individual pericopes—will be observed.

3. Through the utilization of pericopal theology, a christiconic hermeneutic, and the subsequent preaching of an expository sermon series,
a measurable growth in congregational discernment of the divine
demand placed on God's people through the biblical text (i.e., the application) will be observable.

Analysis of the pretest and posttest surveys addressed the research
question presented above, providing quantitative information and data related to each of the three hypotheses guiding this study. Results from the
statistical tests conducted from the data received are presented to illustrate
and give evidence for these findings. The data acquired from the pretest
and posttest surveys was analyzed through a two-tailed paired t-test. The
analysis was paired because the same group was tested both before and after
the expository sermon series (i.e., the independent variable). The analysis
was two-tailed because, in theory, effects of the preaching series could go
in both directions.[1] Obviously, for hearers of an expositional sermon series
to *decrease* in their biblical, theological, and/or applicational understanding
of a passage of Scripture would be a most unfortunate discovery for the
preacher, but the possibility certainly exists. The t-test measured whether
the two means being compared were reliably and significantly different
from one another.

The results indicate that an expository sermon series on the book of
Jonah that utilizes pericopal theology and a christiconic hermeneutic does
indicate associated increases in all three areas tested: (1) growth in biblical
knowledge, (2) growth in theological understanding, and (3) growth in applicational discernment. These associated increases are statistically significant, validated by the P-value of the t-test, which was 0.05, meaning that the
probability that the difference between pretest and posttest means was due
to random chance and therefore unreliable was only 5 percent. The null hypothesis (in this case, that an expository sermon series on the book of Jonah
will *not* demonstrate associated increases in biblical knowledge, theological
understanding, and applicational discernment) is rejected if the P-value is
0.05 or less. Therefore, in this research the null hypothesis *is* rejected, and the
research concludes that an expository sermon series on the book of Jonah
that utilizes pericopal theology and a christiconic hermeneutic *does* demonstrate associated increases in all three hypotheses. Given the P-value of
0.05, the confidence level/interval that the hypotheses are validated by this
data is 95 percent. In the paragraphs that follow, results are presented to give
evidence of associated increases as related to each of the three hypotheses.

1. Frost, "One-Tailed and Two-Tailed," https://statisticsbyjim.com/hypothesis-testing
/one-tailed-two-tailed-hypothesis-tests/.

HYPOTHESIS 1: GROWTH IN BIBLICAL KNOWLEDGE

Explanation of Process

The first hypothesis states that through the utilization of pericopal theology, a christiconic hermeneutic, and the subsequent preaching of an expository sermon series, there will be measurable growth in congregational knowledge of the biblical text. While the research question focused on the preacher's and hearers' discernment of valid applicational truth alone, as was argued and demonstrated in chapter 2 of this project, knowledge of the biblical text (and, in particular, the author's *doings* with his *sayings*) must precede a discernment of its proper application. Thus, it was necessary and advantageous to measure potential growth in biblical knowledge (i.e., how much hearers increased in their knowledge of what the individual pericopes of Jonah include, details about the account, and plot development included by the author). If growth is to be found in a hearer's discernment of valid application of a given pericope, then growth in knowledge of the text from which application is drawn must also be found.

To measure this growth in biblical understanding, the researcher looked at pretest and posttest results flanking an expository sermon series on the book of Jonah related to this particular hypothesis. More specifically, the twelve questions included in the survey that were tailored to this particular end were examined and results compared. The quantitative data collected from this portion of the instrument made it possible to determine whether there was a statistically significant difference between the two test scores for individual participants as well as the group as a whole, thereby affirming the first hypothesis. Table 4.1 provides an overview of the statistics related to the first hypothesis.

Table 4.1. Statistics for Hypothesis 1: Biblical Knowledge			
	Pretest Findings	Posttest Findings	Change
Mean (%)	49 ± 2.3	75 ± 2.6	26 ± 3.5
Observations	65	65	
Degrees of Freedom	64		
t Value	-9.8		
Confidence Level (%)	95		
t Critical Two-Tail	2.0		

Statement of Findings

As stated above, a total of twelve questions were crafted with the express purpose of measuring hypothesis 1. Each question was multiple choice and included six potential answers as described in chapter 3 and as can be seen in appendix C. Participants were given a score of 1 if they selected the correct answer and 0 if they selected one of the other five options. In the case that the participant did not follow the instructions on the survey[2] (e.g., they circled more than one option, left the question blank, etc.) they were given a 0. The maximum score any participant could receive was 12 and, after counting the number of their correct responses, a percentage score was calculated and recorded. This was repeated for the posttest and the two percentages compared.

The mean estimation examined the overall difference in the pretest and posttest scores for the twelve questions related to hypothesis 1 by comparing the score totals from all participants. Measuring the sixty-five participants, the average score on the pretest was 49 percent with the average score on the posttest being 75 percent.

Table 4.2. Graph of Results for Hypothesis 1: Bible Knowledge

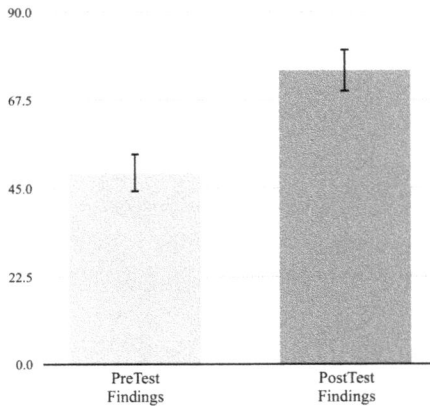

This is a 53 percent increase between the two sets of data. Given the P-value of 0.05, this result is not likely due to chance.[3] The mean estimation for

2. "Without consulting your Bible or any other resource, circle the best answer to the following questions."

3. That is, in 5 percent of cases, due to chance, we would *not* be able to reject the null hypothesis.

biblical knowledge questions validates a significant step toward the research question: Can the implementation of pericopal theology and a christiconic hermeneutic aid in a preacher's identification and communication of valid application and the hearer's comprehension of that application?

The mean estimation shows an overall increase in pretest and post-test scores on questions designed to measure growth in biblical knowledge. This data was acquired by examining the collective data of participants and the questions pertaining to the first hypothesis. Interestingly, when viewed independently, the data indicates that the average score for each and every question increased between the pretest and posttest as well.

Table 4.3. Growth by Question in Hypothesis 1: Biblical Knowledge			
Question	Pretest (%)	Posttest (%)	Change (%)
1	81.5	96.9	18.9
2	13.8	40	189.9
3	41.5	72.3	74.2
7	72.3	80	10.7
8	23.1	44.6	93.1
9	12.3	78.5	538.2
13	63.1	89.2	41.4
14	60	81.5	35.8
15	61.5	84.6	37.6
19	61.5	84.6	37.6
20	38.5	73.8	91.7
21	58.5	73.8	26.2

The first hypothesis can be supported based on the scores from the quantitative research in the sections of the instrument pertaining to that particular hypothesis. The findings indicate that hearers of an expository sermon series that utilizes pericopal theology and a christiconic hermeneutic do in fact demonstrate an associated growth in biblical knowledge of the preached text of Scripture.

HYPOTHESIS 2: GROWTH IN THEOLOGICAL UNDERSTANDING

Explanation of Process

The second hypothesis of the current project is that through the utilization of pericopal theology, a christiconic hermeneutic, and the subsequent preaching of an expository sermon series, a measurable growth in congregational understanding of the *theology* of the pericope will be observed. It should be mentioned again that, while the research question focused on the preacher's and hearers' discernment of valid applicational truth alone, this growth depends not only on biblical knowledge but on theological understanding as well. Said otherwise, one cannot be sure of applicational validity from a text without first understanding the theology of the text (i.e., pericopal theology), and one cannot rightly identify the theology of a text without first understanding the text itself, observing what the author is *doing* with what he is *saying*. Thus, to answer the question guiding this research (hypothesis 3), questions regarding growth in biblical knowledge (hypothesis 1) and theological understanding (hypothesis 2) must first be examined.

To measure this growth in theological understanding, the researcher looked at pretest and posttest results on either side of an expository sermon series on the book of Jonah related to this particular hypothesis. More specifically, the eight questions included in the survey that were tailored to this particular end were examined and the results compared.

The quantitative data collected from this particular portion of the instrument made it possible to determine whether there was a statistically significant difference between the two test scores for individual participants as well as the group as a whole, thereby affirming the second hypothesis. Below in Table 4.4 is an overview of the statistics related to the second hypothesis.

Table 4.4. Statistics for Hypothesis 2: Theological Understanding			
	Pretest Findings	Posttest Findings	Change
Mean (%)	17.7 ± 2.2	50 ± 4.2	32.3 ± 4.7
Observations	65	65	
Degrees of Freedom	64		
t Value	-7.5		
Confidence Level (%)	95		
t Critical Two-Tail	2.0		

Statement of Findings

A total of eight questions were crafted for the purpose of measuring hypothesis 2. Each was multiple choice and included six potential answers as described in chapter 3 and seen in appendix C. The maximum score was 8 and, after counting the number of their correct responses, a percentage score was calculated and recorded. This was repeated for the posttest and the two percentages were compared.

The mean estimation examined the overall difference in the pretest and posttest scores for the eight questions related to hypothesis 2 by comparing the score totals from all participants. Measuring the sixty-five participants, the average score on the pretest was 18 percent with the average score on the posttest being 50 percent. This represents a 178 percent increase between the two sets of data. Given the P-value of 0.05, this result is not likely due to chance.[4] The mean estimation for theological understanding questions validates a significant step toward the research question: Can the implementation of pericopal theology and a christiconic hermeneutic aid in a preacher's identification and communication of valid application and the hearer's comprehension of that application?

Table 4.5. Graph of Results for Hypothesis 2: Theological Understanding

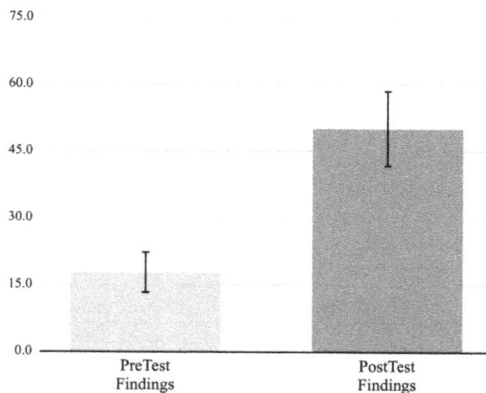

The mean estimation shows an overall increase in pretest and posttest scores on questions designed to measure hypothesis 2 (i.e., growth in theological understanding). This data was acquired by examining the collective

---

4. That is, in 5 percent of cases, due to chance, we would *not* be able to reject the null hypothesis.

data of all participants and all of the questions pertaining to the second hypothesis. When viewed independently, the data indicates that the average score for each and every question increased between the pretest and posttest as well (see Table 4.6 below).

Table 4.6. Growth by Question in Hypothesis 2: Theological Understanding			
Question	Pretest (%)	Posttest (%)	Change (%)
4	21.5	47.7	121.9
5	16.9	55.4	227.8
10	9.2	44.6	384.8
11	4.6	47.7	937.0
16	12.3	35.4	187.8
17	38.5	61.5	59.7
22	16.9	47.7	182.2
23	27.7	53.5	93.1

The second hypothesis can be supported based on the scores from the quantitative research in the sections of the instrument pertaining to this particular hypothesis. The findings indicate that hearers of an expository sermon series that utilizes pericopal theology and a christiconic hermeneutic do in fact demonstrate an associated growth in theological understanding.

HYPOTHESIS 3: GROWTH IN APPLICATIONAL DISCERNMENT

Explanation of Process

The third and final hypothesis of the current project is that through the utilization of pericopal theology, a christiconic hermeneutic, and the subsequent preaching of an expository sermon series, a measurable growth in congregational discernment of the divine demand placed on God's people through the biblical text (i.e., the application) will be observable. This hypothesis strikes at the core of the research question driving the current study: Can the implementation of pericopal theology and a christiconic hermeneutic aid in a preacher's identification and communication of valid application and the hearer's comprehension of that application?

As has already been said, it was necessary to first study and measure the potential growth in biblical knowledge (hypothesis 1) and theological understanding (hypothesis 2) of a passage of Scripture in order to then measure growth in applicational discernment (hypothesis 3). One cannot be confident in what God is calling one to do (i.e., divine demand) in response to a given pericope of Scripture unless the theology of that passage (i.e., pericopal theology) is first rightly discerned and its thrust rightly experienced. And one cannot rightly understand the theology of the pericope unless the text (i.e., authorial *sayings*) is properly observed first. Hypothesis 3, building atop the two previous, finally comes to the applicational question, that of the divine demand placed upon the hearer/reader of the pericope(s) in question.

To measure this growth in applicational understanding, the researcher looked at pretest and posttest results flanking an expository sermon series on the book of Jonah related to this particular hypothesis. More specifically, the four questions included in the survey that were tailored to this particular end were examined and results were compared. The quantitative data collected from this portion of the instrument made it possible to determine whether there was a statistically significant difference between the two test scores for individual participants as well as the group as a whole, thereby affirming the third hypothesis. Below in Table 4.7 is an overview of the statistics related to the third hypothesis.

Table 4.7. Statistics for Hypothesis 3: Applicational Discernment			
	Pretest Findings	Posttest Findings	Change
Mean (%)	10 ± 2.2	51.2 ± 4.7	41.2 ± 5.2
Observations	65	65	
Degrees of Freedom	64		
t Value	-9.0		
Confidence Level (%)	95		
t Critical Two-Tail	2.0		

Statement of Findings

A total of four questions were crafted for the purpose of measuring hypothesis 3. Each was multiple choice and included six potential answers as described in chapter 3 and seen in appendix C. The maximum score was 4 and, after counting the number of their correct responses, a percentage score was calculated and recorded. This was repeated for the posttest and the two percentages were compared.

The mean estimation examined the overall difference in the pretest and posttest scores for the four questions related to hypothesis 3 by comparing the score totals from all participants. Measuring the sixty-five participants, the average score on the pretest was 10 percent with the average score on the posttest being 51 percent. This represents a 410 percent increase from the first set of data to the second data. Given the P-value of 0.05, this result is not likely due to chance.[5] The mean estimation for applicational discernment questions validates the hypothesis that through the utilization of pericopal theology, a christiconic hermeneutic, and the subsequent preaching of an expository sermon series, a measurable growth in congregational discernment of the divine demand placed on God's people through the biblical text (i.e., the application) will be observable.

Table 4.8. Graph of Results for Hypothesis 3: Applicational Discernment

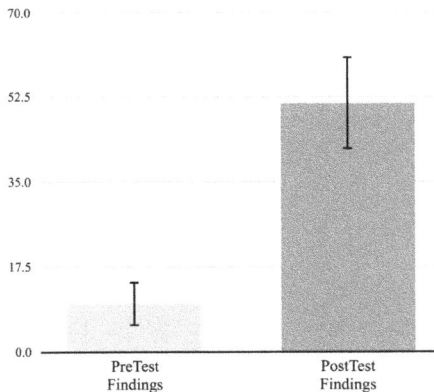

The mean estimation shows an overall increase in pretest and posttest scores on questions designed to measure hypothesis 3 (i.e., growth in applicational discernment). This data was acquired by examining the collective data of all participants and all of the questions pertaining to the third hypothesis. Interestingly, when viewed independently, the data indicates that the average score for each and every question increased between the pretest and posttest as well (see Table 4.9).

5. That is, in 5 percent of cases, due to chance, we would *not* be able to reject the null hypothesis.

Table 4.9. Growth by Question in Hypothesis 3: Applicational Discernment			
Question	Pretest (%)	Posttest (%)	Change (%)
6	12.3	47.7	287.8
12	3.1	52.3	1587.1
18	12.3	55.4	350.4
24	15.4	46.2	200.0

The third hypothesis can be supported based on the scores from the quantitative research in the sections of the instrument pertaining to this particular hypothesis. The findings indicate that hearers of an expository sermon series that utilizes pericopal theology and a christiconic hermeneutic do in fact demonstrate an associated growth in applicational discernment.

CONCLUSION

This research project was undertaken with the ultimate goal of exploring and evaluating the implementation of pericopal theology and a christiconic hermeneutic in the homiletical process. The question asked was: Can the implementation of pericopal theology and a christiconic hermeneutic aid in a preacher's identification and communication of valid application and the hearer's comprehension of that application?

The data collected and analyzed from pretest and posttest results statistically validates all three hypotheses articulated in relation to the above research question. Hearers of an expository sermon series on the book of Jonah, a series of sermons that utilized pericopal theology and a christiconic hermeneutic, show an associated growth in biblical knowledge (i.e., knowledge of what the author is *saying*) (hypothesis 1). This hypothesis was validated in that pretest and posttest scores indicated a statistically significant increase.

Also, hearers of the expository sermon series demonstrate an associated growth in their theological understanding of the passage of Scripture preached (i.e., understanding of what the biblical author is *doing* with what he's *saying* or the *thrust* of the text) (hypothesis 2). This hypothesis was validated by the fact that pretest and posttest scores revealed a statistically significant increase.

Finally, hearers of an expository sermon series that utilized both a pericopal theology and a christiconic hermeneutic demonstrated an associated growth in applicational discernment (i.e., the *divine demand* God is placing upon his people by and through the text in question) (hypothesis

3). This hypothesis was validated by the pretest and posttest results, which yielded a statistically significant increase.

The growth associated with all three hypotheses is presented together for ease of visual comparison in Table 4.10 below. While growth is apparent in each of the three pairs of tests, viewing them side by side shows the relatively dramatic growth in the latter two, particularly the final pair (i.e., applicational discernment).

Table 4.10. Composite Graph of Results for All Hypotheses

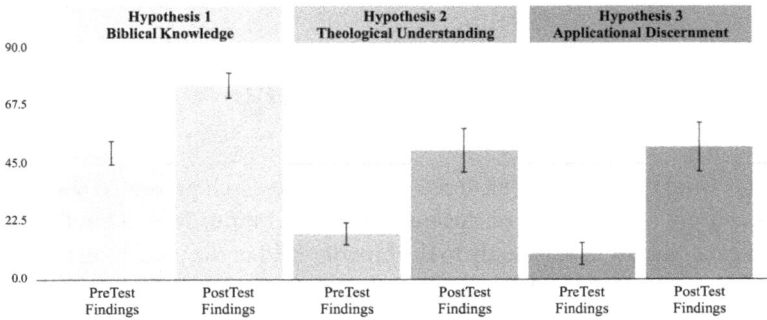

5

Implications of the Findings

THIS CONCLUDING CHAPTER SUMMARIZES the research presented above and draws from it defensible conclusions for consideration. Several implications and generalizations that apply to the broader field of the preaching ministry are suggested as well. Also included in this final section are a number of recommendations for further study that may provide meaningful direction for subsequent students, researchers, and theologians.

INTRODUCTION AND SUMMARY

As was outlined and articulated in chapter 1, this research project was undertaken with the ultimate goal of exploring and evaluating the implementation of pericopal theology and a christiconic hermeneutic in the homiletical process. Particular attention was given to the development and communication of valid application of specific biblical pericopes characterized by clear and observable fidelity to the Scriptures and biblically supportable, modern-day relevance for the hearers. To this end, exegetical and theological work was done in the book of Jonah, a corresponding four-week expository sermon series was prepared and preached, and a self-administered pretest and posttest survey was distributed to voluntary participants, the majority of whom were members of Oakridge Bible Chapel (OBC) in Oakville, Ontario, Canada. The survey, identical in both distributions, focused on the content of the text, i.e., what the author is *saying*, the theology of the four pericopes of the book of Jonah, i.e., what the author is *doing* with what he's saying (the *thrust* and *divine demand* therein), and their practical implications for God's people today, i.e., the *applicational command* of the text(s). The data was then analyzed against the three hypotheses, validating the hypotheses or refining them to accurately reflect the trends revealed in the collected surveys.

The literature review in chapter 2 attempted to situate the current study in the field of homiletics as it currently stands. There is widespread agreement that a vital facet of corporate worship for God's people is God's word preached—and preached *well*—and that a vital element of biblical preaching is the development and communication of valid application as Scripture itself claims that its application is expected (Matt 7:24; Luke 6:46–47; Rom 15:4; Jas 1:22). It is the task of the preacher, then, to guide God's people from the *then* of the text to the *now* of today, helping them rightly apply God's word in a way consistent with authorial intent.

Unfortunately, to date little has been written regarding the process by which any preacher can make this homiletical leap and develop *valid* application (observably biblical and exegetically traceable) for their people. The goal is faithful, biblical, text-driven exegesis that allows for valid, comprehendible, and relevant application, but there is a dearth in the literature, it would seem, of aid for preachers in this very important task.

Abraham Kuruvilla's pericopal theology and christiconic hermeneutic is an interpretive approach that may address some of the concerns that exist in previous methodologies (e.g., christocentric interpretation) and attempts to remove the seemingly subjective components of moving from text to praxis. By privileging the text and sitting under preaching that utilizes a theological hermeneutic, God's people will not only be able to better understand what God is *saying* semantically, but they will be able to discern what God is *doing* pragmatically with what he is saying. When these two realities are understood and seen in the inspired text itself, valid application can be heard with confidence and applied with conviction.

With such an important and perennial need left wanting (i.e., a way of moving from text to valid application that is objectively biblical) and with a potential method of meeting this need suggested by the work of Kuruvilla, the goal of the current study was to investigate its effectiveness. This aim is reflected in the research question: Can the implementation of pericopal theology and a christiconic hermeneutic aid in a preacher's identification and communication of valid application and the hearer's comprehension of that application? In other words, and more broadly, can and should the hermeneutics and homiletics community accept and celebrate the steps forward that have been charted by Kuruvilla in the long-attempted and long-needed bridging of the chasm between text and praxis, exegesis and application?

Informed and enhanced by the literature, a sermon series was developed on the book of Jonah. Approaching the text using pericopal theology and a christiconic hermeneutic as articulated, demonstrated, and modeled by Kuruvilla himself, this book of the Bible was translated, mapped, scripted, and preached. The goal was to, through theological exegesis, determine the *thrust* of each pericope of Jonah as well as the divine demand therein. Through the preaching of the text, then, the researcher sought to curate for his congregation the four pericopes of Jonah, demonstrating the authorial intent and leading them as a group toward the discernment of valid application. The assumption was that, with this methodology being demonstrated for them, the people of God would be able to understand the book of Jonah in greater ways, not only biblically, but theologically and in terms of applicability as well.

In order to move from assumption to assessment, an instrument was developed to measure the hypotheses that predicted positive results in each of those three areas of investigation—growth in biblical knowledge, theological understanding, and applicational discernment of the text of Jonah. The instrument developed was a self-administered survey distributed, completed, and submitted both before and after the sermon series on the book of Jonah. Eighty-one individuals participated in the first round of surveys with sixty-five returning to participate in the second round. The results of the pretest were analyzed in comparison to the results of the posttest. This data was evaluated through a t-test yielding data that validated each of the three hypotheses. Hearers of the sermon series demonstrated associated growth in biblical knowledge, theological understanding, and, ultimately, applicational discernment of the biblical account of Jonah. The process of survey development and the results of the study are found in chapters 3 and 4 respectively.

INTERPRETATION OF RESULTS AND CONCLUSIONS

The foremost conclusion drawn from the current study is that preaching expository sermons that implement pericopal theology and a christiconic hermeneutic is an effective means of encouraging hearers to grow in their biblical knowledge, theological understanding, and applicational discernment of the Scriptures. An examination of the quantitative information and data from this applied research project supports the finding that such preaching and such sermons positively affect the ability of participants to understand what the biblical author is *saying* and *doing* (with what he is *saying*) and, ultimately, what God wants *them* to do in response.

As the analysis displayed in chapter 4 indicates, there were discernible and statistically significant differences in the participants' development in each area. Table 5.1 below summarizes the data collected from the research organized by the three hypotheses, the mean response for both the pretest and posttest, and the change observed between the two.

Table 5.1. Summary of Research Results			
	Pretest Findings	Posttest Findings	Total Increase
Biblical Knowledge *Authorial Sayings*	49 ± 2.3	75 ± 2.6	53
Theological Understanding *Pericopal Theology, Authorial Doings*	17.7 ± 2.2	50 ± 4.2	182.5
Applicational Discernment *Appropriate Calls to Action*	10 ± 2.2	51.2 ± 4.7	412

Conclusions Regarding Hypothesis 1

While the research question driving this study focused on the determination and discernment of valid application of a biblical text, it was important to first determine whether the utilization of pericopal theology and a christiconic hermeneutic affected hearer's knowledge of the biblical text. As has already been discussed, it is only with appropriate biblical knowledge (i.e., observing the text itself) that one can then obtain right theological understanding, a prerequisite for the discernment of valid application.

It was for this reason that hypothesis 1 was the following: Through the utilization of pericopal theology, a christiconic hermeneutic, and the subsequent preaching of an expository sermon series, there will be measurable growth in congregational knowledge of the biblical text. The research instrument provided quantitative data making it possible to determine whether there was a statistically significant difference between pretest and posttest scores.

With the expository sermon series serving as the independent variable, the differences in the pretest and posttest scores highlighted growth in connection with the preaching. The mean estimation examined the overall difference in pretest and posttest scores for questions tailored specifically to address hypothesis 1 by comparing the score totals from all participants. Measuring the total sixty-five participants, the average score on the pretest was 49 percent, the average posttest score was 75 percent, and the increase

between the two was 53 percent. The mean scores for the biblical understanding questions made it possible to conclude that hearers of expository
preaching that implements pericopal theology and a christiconic hermeneutic demonstrate an increase in biblical knowledge (i.e., understanding
authorial *sayings*).

Observations Regarding Growth in Biblical Knowledge

The acceptance of hypothesis 1 in the current study will not surprise most.
It makes sense that in listening to a sermon series on a particular passage of
Scripture or book of the Bible hearers would grow in their knowledge of what
the author of this biblical text describes. In the case of Jonah, hearers grew
in clarity as to all that was involved in the account, the order in which the
account is recorded, in what ways God corrected and rebuked his prophet,
and the motivation the text describes for Jonah's retreat from his God.

The fact that hypothesis 1 revealed the lowest increase of the three—
a 53 percent change between the pretest and posttest as compared to 178
percent for hypothesis 2 and 410 percent for hypothesis 3—is also not surprising. This may be explained by a brief examination of the demographics
of the participants, contributing to a relatively high score on the pretest
on questions regarding biblical knowledge. Participants of this study self-
reported as being not only members of a church family that, for decades, has
dedicated itself to Bible teaching, but regular attenders of that church (97
percent anonymously reported attending "basically every Sunday"). Also,
82 percent of participants were over the age of forty-five, 89 percent had
been Christians for at least fifteen years, 85 percent for at least twenty years.
Thus, it is not a leap to assume that this particular participant pool had a
higher-than-average grasp of the Bible in general and good foundational
knowledge of the account of Jonah in particular. In fact, if another book
of the Bible had been used for this project, base knowledge would have
likely been high as well. It should be noted that there was still a significant
increase in Bible knowledge, regardless of a high starting point, but this,
again, is expected when sitting under Bible-based preaching, regardless of
methodology. This observation also serves to highlight the effectiveness of
the methodology being studied as particularly helpful in regard to the second and third hypotheses.

A total of twelve questions on the survey were designed to measure
the growth of hearer's biblical knowledge, three for each pericope of Jonah.
While many details could have been included from each section of the biblical text to measure this growth, details specific to the thrust of that pericope

were chosen as hypothesis 2 measured the theology of the pericopes and such details are important for *thrust* identification. For example, question 2 asked: "What was Jonah's stated motivation for disobeying God in chapter 1?" The correct answer, the answer the text itself provides the attentive reader and preacher, is "Fleeing from God's presence" (Jonah 1:3[x2], 10). Privileging the text means just that and the avoidance of importing assumed or hypothesized motivations. Understanding that it was the very *presence* of the Lord this *prophet* of the Lord was fleeing, a motive he apparently shared with the pagan sailors on whose ship he was attempting said retreat, is crucial for understanding the theological focus of the pericope: "God's people obediently reflect his compassionate character to those around them and, in so doing, avoid descending from, *not his presence* but, his blessings."[1]

Another example is found in question 9: "What is the emotional tenor of Jonah 2? In other words, according to the text, what is the best description of the prophet's mood and/or heart condition at this point of the story?" Without a hearer understanding from the text itself that Jonah's prayer is one of self-righteousness and hypocrisy, the thrust of the text will be missed and, ultimately, valid application will be impossible. Again, while it is not surprising that expositional preaching has a positive effect on hearers' knowledge of the text being brought before them, it is an important and foundational reality that must be measured in order to eventually observe the effect of the preaching of the word of God on hearers' understanding of theology and discernment of its application.

An obvious conclusion regarding the first hypothesis of this study is that preaching the word of God leads to greater biblical knowledge in those who sit under such sermons. When a preacher stands before God's people, opens the biblical text, reads the biblical text, and explains the biblical text, God's people grow in their knowledge of the biblical text. While not a novel assertion, the current study does provide support for what is often considered an assumption. When the psalmist prays, "Teach me your way, O Lord; I will walk in your truth" (Ps 86:11), he assumes that God's truth is knowable, understandable, and accessible. When the apostle John, likewise, states in celebration, "I have no greater joy than this, to hear of my children walking in the truth" (3 John 1:4), he assumes the same. Preachers of God's word desire God to teach his people his ways so that they may walk in his truth. To this end, preachers must teach God's truth. This study indicates that when they do this, hearers grow in their understanding of what that truth is, increasing their capacity for walking in it.

---

1. Emphasis added. See appendix A for more details.

Conclusions Regarding Hypothesis 2

Again, while this study's research question focused on the determination and discernment of valid application of a biblical text, it was important to first determine whether the utilization of pericopal theology and a christiconic hermeneutic effected hearers' biblical knowledge (hypothesis 1) and theological understanding (hypothesis 2). As has already been discussed, it is only with appropriate biblical knowledge that anyone can then obtain right theological understanding, which is, in turn, a prerequisite for the discernment of valid application.

It was for this reason that hypothesis 2 was the following: Through the utilization of pericopal theology, a christiconic hermeneutic, and the subsequent preaching of an expository sermon series, a measurable growth in congregational understanding of the *theology* of the biblical text will be observed. The research instrument provided quantitative data making it possible to determine whether there was a statistically significant difference between pretest and posttest scores in this area.

With the expository sermon series serving as the independent variable, the differences in the pretest and posttest scores highlighted growth in connection with the preaching. The mean estimation examined the overall difference in pretest and posttest scores for questions tailored specifically to address hypothesis 2 by comparing the score totals from all participants. Measuring the total sixty-five participants, the average score on the pretest was 18 percent with the average posttest score being 50 percent, an increase of 178 percent. Thus, the mean scores for theological understanding questions made it possible to conclude that hearers of expository preaching implementing pericopal theology and a christiconic hermeneutic demonstrate an increase in theological understanding (i.e., authorial *doings*).

Observations Regarding Growth in Theological Understanding

As was discussed in the literature review in chapter 2, the identification of authorial *doings* with authorial *sayings* is crucial for the development of valid application (i.e., application consistent with the desire[s] of the communicator). This is true of all communication and not only God's communication to his people through his word. A teacher's communication toward a student, "The door is open," has multiple potential interpretations. Is the student being told to *leave* the classroom? Perhaps she is being prompted to come *into* the classroom? Or is the student being given an explanation as to why it is so loud in the room? Perhaps the teacher is simply reporting her accessibility to her student, akin to "I'm always available." For the student hearing the utterance of the teacher, an understanding of the communicator's intentions with the words he has chosen is paramount if valid application is to be identified and acted upon.

So too with the biblical text. God has spoken that his people may know him and be conformed into the image of his Son through obedience to his word and by the power of the Holy Spirit. And, since all Scripture is breathed out by God and useful to those ends, all passages of Holy Writ are divine utterances, the thrust of which must be discerned (i.e., the theology of the pericope understood) if application consistent with God's intention is to be discerned and lived out. Assuming the pastor has rightly identified the theology of the passage being preached, it must be communicated to his hearers in such a way that it is clearly seen coming up out of the text itself.

In the current study, participants showed an increased ability to understand the theology of the four pericopes of Jonah. This is an important intermediary step between the text and faithful praxis. It was encouraging to see participants grow in their ability to rightly identify the thrust and *divine demand* of the biblical text, particularly in light of the other options with which they were presented. As was briefly discussed earlier in this project, many popular approaches to biblical interpretation and application today involve methodologies that, from this researcher's point of view, are difficult to support biblically, superficial in their postulations, and mysterious in their movements. Many of these types of methodologies were used to populate the pretest and posttest survey and surround the correct answer.

For example, question 16 asked: "What best describes the main point, *thrust*, or focus that God is communicating through the text of Jonah 3? (Note: While all below statements may be taught in the Bible, not all are the primary teaching of this particular chapter.)" One of the options provided for the participants' consideration was: "God, being gracious and loving, desires his message of reconciliation to spread to *all* nations, a desire that found its full realization in the gospel of Jesus Christ." This possible answer utilizes a christocentric view of biblical interpretation. In considering the whole of the biblical canon, the above statement could be affirmed. However, when paying attention to the theology of the pericope of Jonah 3, there is no mention of the gospel of salvation by grace through faith (implied) or of Jesus Christ. Another possible answer to that same question was: "The gospel, a message powerful enough to change lives eternally, is surprisingly simple and understandable." This option, similar to the last, takes a soteriological view of all Scripture. Again, while not an incorrect statement, it is not one that can be supported from the pericope in question.

A similar strategy was used in the questions regarding the divine demand in each pericope. That participants in this study were able to grow in their understanding of the theology of the pericopes is encouraging. It seems they increased in their ability to wade through a number of generally true statements and identify the one that is true for the text in question. This no doubt is related to their growth in biblical knowledge and lays important groundwork for potential growth in applicational discernment.

Conclusions Regarding Hypothesis 3

The research question driving this current study was concerned with the growth of discernment of valid application for God's people. Through an expository sermon series that utilized pericopal theology and a christiconic hermeneutic, would hearers grow in their ability to identify and understand the applicational command of individual pericopes of Scripture, applications rooted in the theology of the pericopes, and in observations of the biblical text itself? Hypothesis 3, standing atop hypotheses 2 and 1 respectively, sought to address this primary question.

It was for this reason that hypothesis 3 was the following: Through the utilization of pericopal theology, a christiconic hermeneutic, and the subsequent preaching of an expository sermon series, a measurable growth in congregational discernment of the *applicational command* placed on God's people through the biblical text (i.e., the application) will be observable. The research instrument provided quantitative data making it possible to determine whether there was a statistically significant difference between pretest and posttest scores in this area.

With the expository sermon series serving as the independent variable, the differences in the pretest and posttest scores highlighted growth in connection with the preaching. The mean estimation examined the overall difference in pretest and posttest scores for questions tailored specifically to address hypothesis 3 by comparing the score totals from all participants. Measuring the total of sixty-five participants, the average score on the pretest was 10 percent with the average posttest score being 51 percent. This is a 410 percent increase between the two. Thus, the mean scores for applicational discernment questions made it possible to conclude that hearers of expository preaching implementing pericopal theology and a christiconic hermeneutic demonstrate an increase in applicational discernment (i.e., the *applicational command* placed by God upon his people).

Observations Regarding Growth in Applicational Understanding

How can an individual read a passage of Scripture and then, with confidence, live out what God is calling them to do therein? This question becomes increasingly important when one understands that God, the divine author, has something specific in mind in each pericope of Scripture, like the teacher mentioned above who tells a student, "The door is open." There are many potential understandings of that utterance, but not just any application will do. What the author/speaker is *doing* with what he is *saying* is crucial to discern if satisfactory application is to be carried out.

God has spoken that his people will listen, obey, and, in so doing, be conformed incrementally to the image of his Son. The book of Jonah is included in that speaking and in that purpose. But how? A quick perusal of any sermon collection website will be demonstration enough that the variety of application suggested by many preachers from the little book of Jonah is wide indeed. Are they all valid? Are all of those suggested applications (i.e., the preacher declaring for God's people, "God wants us to do this") rightly understanding God's desired intention for his people? It should be clear that not all can be right. It is the understanding of this researcher that a valid application must be rooted in the *divine demand* of the passage of Scripture in question. That *divine demand* must grow out of the *thrust* of the text, a thrust best discerned through the utilization of pericopal theology and a christiconic hermeneutic, a method of interpretation that privileges the text of Scripture.

Participants in this study, after hearing a series of sermons on the book of Jonah that utilized pericopal theology and a christiconic hermeneutic, showed significant growth in both their biblical knowledge and their theological understanding of the text taught. These are two steps that *must* be in place if growth in applicational discernment can be found. Noteworthily, that is exactly what was observed. Participants increased in their ability to identify an appropriate applicational command in the midst of five other legitimate-sounding suggestions.

For example, question 12 asked: "Understanding the *thrust* and *divine demand* of Jonah 2, what is the most appropriate *applicational command* for God's people today?" The way the question is asked, the connection of application to theology is immediately apparent. Also, of the potential answers offered, all were crafted to sound biblical, God honoring, and worthy of consideration. However, the question is: Which is valid *from the second chapter of Jonah*, considering the theology of the pericope curated for the hearer in the sermon on that passage? "Trust God always!" sounds appropriate and is certainly a biblical command. "When in deep, call to be lifted up!" is pithy and speaks to the descent of Jonah into the sea and the prayers he offers up to God, but assumes a positive understanding of chapter 2, one that this researcher is unconvinced that the text itself supports. As one can imagine, even those two different applicational commands will lead a hearer in two different directions when it comes to application, and they cannot both be valid from the text. That the participants of this study were able to grow in their ability to understand not only the biblical text itself but also its theology and applicational properties is celebratory.

LIMITATIONS

The findings of this research project indicate statistically significant data regarding the associated growth that came as a result of an expositional sermon series utilizing pericopal theology and a christiconic hermeneutic. The P-value of 0.05 allows for a high probability of 95 percent that the data is reliable and not based on random chance. Since these statistics are inferential, similar results could be expected in new samples. However, there are limits to this statement, some of which are explored in the following paragraphs.

While the findings of this study are statistically significant, confidence could always be increased with a larger sample size. In the current study, sixty-five individuals voluntarily participated. The vast majority of these were from OBC, a church that has a wide range of ethnic and denominational backgrounds represented. This variety could at least partially be attributed to its location—the Greater Toronto Area, a significant multicultural city center. However, even with the advantages of the sample used, a higher number of participants would have been advantageous.

In addition to the number of participants being a potential limitation of the current study, greater demographic diversity in certain areas would have likewise been helpful. For example, only two participants reported to be under the age of twenty-five and only twelve reported being under the age of forty-five. This means that 82 percent of those participating in this study were forty-five and older. With a more diversified sample in regard to age, more analysis could have been done on youth, young adults, and young families and how each of these groups are impacted by the preaching methodology used in this study in terms of their understanding of the Bible, its theology, and its applicability. Other demographical information could also have been helpful to collect from participants (e.g., marital status, ethnicity, denominational background, etc.) as the population of the geographical area in which OBC is situated is quite diverse.

Perhaps related to the age category was the self-reported number of years each participant had been a Christian. Fifty-five out of sixty-five reported being a Christian for at least twenty years. There are many questions that arise with this measure. After twenty years, do these participants start at a much higher level of understanding when it comes to the measured categories? Or, perhaps they are, after so much church attendance, more ingrained in a specific way of reading, understanding, and applying the Bible that would be difficult to unlearn. Without greater diversity in Christian experience, these questions are left unanswered.

Another possible limitation of the study was the length and comprehensiveness of the tool used for data collection. As was explained in chapter 3, the intention was to create a tool that was both usable (i.e., not overwhelmingly long and complicated) as well as helpful in exploring the three hypotheses. However, a twenty-five-question survey can only provide so much data and can only cover a limited amount of the biblical text. This shortcoming was perhaps most pronounced in the questions regarding the applicational command of each pericope. Space only permitted a single question per pericope/sermon and limited attention as to how an individual understood how the text, its theology, and its application are related. The commitment to quantitative data could also be seen as a limitation. Whereas qualitative information may have better filled in some of the blanks as to how participants traced a biblical authors' *sayings* and *doings*, analysis would have changed significantly as well.

Another potential limitation of the current study was the lack of a control group against which the methodology being measured and observed could be directly compared. It has been demonstrated in this study that a sermon series utilizing pericopal theology and a christiconic hermeneutic leads to growth in biblical, theological, and applicational understanding. However, would there have been similar growth—at least in one or two of those categories (perhaps in hypothesis 1)—if, say, a redemptive-historical hermeneutic were used? The correlation has certainly been established between the sermon series delivered and the participants who heard it, but there is no comparative group who sat under a sermon series using an alternative methodology. Ultimately, there was no control group that could increase the confidence that it was indeed the pericopal theology and christiconic hermeneutic responsible for the change observed.

Because of the close proximity of the pretest and posttest surveys to the sermon series, a potential limitation is that participants simply regurgitated what they had memorized from the individual messages presented rather than understood the movement from text to praxis being demonstrated. On one hand, this concern may be moot as it *is* the pastor who is charged with the task of feeding the sheep under his care. On the other hand, the current study was unable to measure whether what was done in the pastor's study was noticed, understood, and could be replicated by the hearers. This may not be so important when members of OBC sit down to have their personal Bible study (i.e., it may be unrealistic and unnecessary to expect them to replicate at home what their pastor does in his study), but it becomes more important when considering their identification of inappropriate Bible study, theological assertions, and applicational demands laid upon them from other teachers. The current research project is limited in its ability to measure the level at which participants understood *why* an applicational command is valid and *why* others are not.

It should also be noted that the sermon series was prepared and preached by one preacher. It would be helpful to conduct the same research with a different preacher or multiple preachers. If, as Kuruvilla asserts, the text of Scripture can only mean what it means, and if pastors study in such a way as to privilege the text, then, in an ideal world, all preachers would, through theological exegesis, arrive at comparable iterations of the theology of the text, its *thrust*, and its *divine demand*. This would be confirmed if other preachers repeated the process outlined in this study. However, every preacher has their own personality, communication style, and personal limitations. As such, the participants of this study were exposed to a single combination of the above. If a variety of preachers were studying and teaching using pericopal theology and a christiconic hermeneutic, the research might indicate different test scores and, at the very least, would add to the robustness of the results obtained and the effectiveness of the methodology in question.

A final limitation to be considered is the unique season in which this current study was carried out. In 2020, the COVID-19 virus swept the globe, shutting down many businesses, organizations, and ministries. Churches were obviously not immune to the subsequent restrictions and OBC was no exception.

In the months prior to the study taking place, the church was closed entirely, unable to meet, and using prerecorded videos to disseminate Sunday teaching. By the time the research was set to begin, the church had begun to gather again, but in limited numbers, in a unique setup, and with many regular congregants unable to attend for a variety of reasons. Because of this reality, the survey was announced, distributed, and collected in a variety of ways, both electronically and in person. Also, the actual sermon series on Jonah was both prerecorded and distributed electronically as well as delivered live for those able and willing to gather.

At the time, OBC was not equipped to livestream its services, thus necessitating the two different preaching moments. Because of the different delivery times (the video was recorded on Wednesday mornings) and the different means of delivery, the two sermons were noticeably different. While the text, exegesis, thrust, divine demand, and applicational command were present in both, the live delivery was longer and more tailored to those gathered. While it is not being stated that one medium is superior for the communication of biblical truth, it should be acknowledged that they *are* different, and some participants only had access to one. However, being forced online in unprecedented ways also expanded the scope of potential participants beyond the walls of OBC.

IMPLICATIONS FOR MINISTRY

Pericopal Theology and a Christiconic Hermeneutic Are Ideal

If the word of God's self-stated goal is the conformation of the people of God to the image of the Son of God, then the preacher's task is to facilitate such work. The people of God *must* grow in their understanding of what it is God has said about himself, his world, his people, his work, his grace, and his expectations. To that end, the text of Scripture must be read and explained. If the people of God are to rightly apply the word of God, they must first know what it says, understand what it is calling them to do, and see how their conformity to its demands—by the power of the Holy Spirit—ushers them another step toward the goal of Christlikeness, as it is only the person of Jesus Christ who has perfectly fulfilled each and every divine demand of Scripture.

The above task is best accomplished through the utilization of pericopal theology and a christiconic hermeneutic. In fact, rightly applying the word of God necessitates rightly understanding its theology (i.e., what God is *doing* with what he's saying). And rightly understanding a passage's theology necessitates rightly understanding the privileged text itself (i.e., what God is *saying*). Thus, to sidestep any facet of this equation is to sacrifice the potential for valid application. It has been the argument of this project that it is pericopal theology that best accomplishes the type of preaching most suited to the curation of the theology of the text and the articulation of valid application that, ultimately, shepherds God's people incrementally toward the image of God's Son by the power of God's Spirit and for God's glory.

Preachers Must Privilege the Text of Scripture

It is not uncommon today for a biblical or systematic theology or hermeneutical presupposition to be privileged rather than the biblical text. Many are taught (and teach) that the text is to be read, studied, and mined for its truths *through* a specific lens worn by the expositor and that it is only through that lens that the text is rightly understood. A christocentric hermeneutic, for example, demands that all pericopes of Scripture must be related to the person and work of Christ. That decision has been made by the preacher before he even comes to the text and, because of that, it drives his exegesis. Jonah 2, therefore, is unable to simply speak for itself and give an example of hypocritical prayer by a prophet who should have known better but must be shoehorned and creatively manipulated to reveal the second person of the Godhead. Two grievous errors simultaneously occur when this takes place: (1) the authorial intent is ignored, missed, or sidestepped; and (2) a non-authorial intent is communicated in its stead. So, not only do the hearers miss what God wants them to hear, but they are force-fed that which he did not intend. When this takes place, valid application simply cannot be obtained and, thus, the very purpose for which the text was given is voided.

The remedy for this common error is a theological exegesis that privileges the text. This does not ignore biblical and systematic theologies but uses them as guardrails ensuring the preacher stays on the road of orthodoxy. Preachers must allow the text to speak, curate its theology for the people, highlight its *divine demand*, and offer valid and appropriate applicational commands from God to God's people.

Preachers Must Give Specific Application

As much as the current study has shown an exciting trend when it comes to the effect of preaching on hearers' ability to know the Bible, understand its theology, and discern its intended application, the numbers are simply not high enough. Even after the sermon series in Jonah, participants scored 75 percent, 50 percent, and 51 percent respectively on questions regarding the *sayings, doings*, and application of those given texts. Again, the improvement is significant, but celebration should not eclipse the fact that even immediately after a sermon series half the participants were still unable to identify the theology and application of the text of Jonah. Granted, this may say more about the preacher than the hearers, but it is regardless a statistic that should raise homiletical eyebrows.

As has been discussed in this work, the application of the word of God to the lives of the people of God is paramount, and in fact is the self-stated *telos* of Scripture. While believers in the congregation have varied levels of Bible knowlege and perhaps have even less theological understanding and ability to discern valid application, it is incumbent upon the preacher to aid them in this process from the pulpit each and every week. Preachers must not only explain the text of Scripture (Bible knowledge) and demonstrate for the people what the biblical authors are *doing* with what they are saying (theological understanding), but they must also help the people rightly bring the word to bear on their lives (applicational discernment). This calls for specific application and not vague implication. The hearer of a sermon should leave knowing exactly what they are being called to do by God and why they are being called to do it.

IMPLICATIONS FOR FUTURE RESEARCH

As noted previously in this chapter, there were certain limitations in this study that leave opportunity for further research. This project could be repeated in order to compare the mean scores reported above and increase the robustness of its claims. Research could also be repeated with a larger sample size and more diversity in the categories of age and years of Christian experience. One could also, with a larger sample size, measure the growth in understanding along the lines of formal theological education, assuming that the more such education one has, the greater their biblical and theological knowledge will be to begin with. Research could also be done concerning the effect of the medium of sermon delivery on the retention and comprehension of the sermon content. The possibilities seem nearly endless. However, all of these are secondary to the following areas in terms of importance for future research.

One of the major barriers to the propagation of the theology and hermeneutic studied in this project is its relative novelty. As was outlined in chapter 2, for a long time those involved in the task of preaching have sought an objective, concrete, communicable, and biblical way to move from text to theology to application. There have been very few significant efforts to articulate this very important homiletical move. Instead, many works on hermeneutics and preaching stop short of recommending how preachers can make this move in such a way as to ensure validity. Many preaching textbooks, if mentioning the move to application at all, describe it as a sort of leap of faith, often rooted in nothing more than a passable literary connection to the text from which it supposedly sprang. The need is very high for: (1) someone to call attention to the piles of invalid applications being offered due to this missing link and label them as the dangers they are, and (2) a robust, biblically saturated, and theologically consistent method of deriving application that is valid.

In the last decade, Abraham Kuruvilla has attempted to meet both of those needs. However, his work is largely buried under a heap of faulty practices and methods that continue because of their momentum and familiarity and in spite of their insecurity and incapability to do what they supposedly are meant to do. Thus, more research needs to be done in the field of language philosophy and pragmatics, work that will supplement Kuruvilla's own and propel it increasingly into the forefront of the collective homiletical mind. No doubt, time will aid in this effort, but more workers will also contribute to its familiarity and implementation.

A more specific and practical way forward in this regard is to continue the work that Kuruvilla has begun in the commentaries he has produced. In his works on the books of Genesis, Judges, Mark, Ephesians, 1–2 Timothy, and Titus, Kuruvilla not only explains and defends pericopal theology and a christiconic hermeneutic, but he also models its usefulness and helpfulness for pastors, preachers, and other communicators of God's word. As one makes their way through his commentaries, this methodology can be seen implemented in real time. As preachers make use of his commentaries in their study, congregations will be met with pericopal theology and the confidence in biblical application it produces. More work needs to be done to help Kuruvilla propagate such work throughout the rest of the canon.

CONCLUSION

This research project developed an expository sermon series on the book of Jonah utilizing pericopal theology and a christiconic hermeneutic and measured its effectiveness to impact hearer growth in biblical, theological, and applicational understanding. It was hypothesized that hearers of the sermon series would increase in all three areas: in their understanding of the book of Jonah (i.e., what the author is *saying*), in their understanding of the theology of the book of Jonah (i.e., what the author is *doing* with what he is saying—the *thrust* and *divine demand* of the pericopes), and in their understanding of the applicability of the pericopes of Jonah (i.e., the *applicational command* placed upon them by God). The method chosen for this research project was a program development and evaluation. Informed by the literature and consultation with the originator of pericopal theology and the christiconic hermeneutic, Abraham Kuruvilla, the text of Jonah was studied using theological exegesis, theological foci were articulated, sermon maps were developed, and sermon manuscripts prepared with the intention of preaching this series to the members of OBC in Oakville, Ontario, Canada.

In order to measure the effectiveness of this sermon series, and the methodology it showcased, on associated growth in the areas hypothesized, an instrument was developed and implemented as a pretest/posttest survey. The instrument provided quantitative data that was analyzed and evaluated in this project. The data verified all three of the hypotheses and, thereby, affirmed that a sermon series on the book of Jonah utilizing pericopal theology and a christiconic hermeneutic demonstrated an associated growth in biblical, theological, and applicational understanding in the participants. This claim was validated and shown to be statistically significant.

For God's people to apply God's word—the self-proclaimed reason for which it was given—they must understand what it is God is calling them to do from each passage of Scripture. To understand what God is calling them to do, they must understand both what God is *saying* and what he is *doing* with what he is saying. Until the theology of any given pericope is rightly discerned, there can be no confidence that the application being offered is valid. Pericopal theology and a christiconic hermeneutic privilege the text in exegesis, highlight its theological thrust, and allow for the identification of valid, text-supported application.

Appendix A

Theological Foci for the Four Pericopes of Jonah

THE FOLLOWING PAGES PROVIDE the theological focus of each of the four pericopes of the book of Jonah as well as suggested subfoci that inform the sermon maps (see appendix B). With the goal being to be as comprehensive as possible, accounting for every major element of the text, these foci are necessarily long and pedantic. Thus, an abridged version, more helpful for the purpose of sermon crafting and preaching, is also offered. Finally, based upon the theological focus of each pericope, an applicational command is suggested.

PERICOPE 1

Reflecting God's Compassion . . . Obediently (Jonah 1)

[God commissions Jonah; Jonah flees from God's presence; The storm and the sailors]

Theological focus[1] of pericope 1

1   Rebellion against God's command that his people reflect his compassionate character to others—even the "evil" and the "outsider"—is to descend from, not his presence but, the blessings of divine usefulness, physical safety, and faithful witness (1:1–17).

   1.1   God commands his people to act as reflective agents of his compassionate character to others, even those we may label as undeserving.

   1.2   Though rebellion may motivate God's people to flee from his presence and, thus, accountability to his commands, God is inescapable.

   1.3   To rebel against God's command to reflect his compassionate character to others—even the perceived undeserved—is to forfeit divine blessing.

Theological focus of pericope 1 for preaching

1   God's people obediently reflect his compassionate character to those around them and, in so doing, avoid descending from, not his presence but, his blessings.

Applicational command of pericope 1

1   Obey and enjoy![2]

---

1. Moving from text to valid application must go through pericopal theology as has been discussed and described in this work. The first step in this direction is to discern the theology of the text/pericope (i.e., what the author is *doing* with what he is *saying*). The Theological Focus, then, is "a single integrated sentence" that is "a label for the authorial *doing* in the text, the pericopal theology." Abraham Kuruvilla, *A Manual for Preaching: The Journey from Text to Sermon* (Grand Rapids, MI: Baker Academic, 2019), 40.

2. For specific application that was given to the people of OBC, see the manuscript of this sermon in Appendix B.

PERICOPE 2

Reflecting God's Compassion . . . Consistently (Jonah 2)

[The belly of the fish; A pseudo-psalm; Jonah's return to land]

Theological focus of pericope 2

2   Prayers that are offered to a God who desires his compassionate character be made known to all but are marked by hypocritical self-concern, misplaced blame, ostentatious promises, and blind prejudices betray the ungodly agenda of the one offering them (2:1–10).

> 2.1   Prayers marked by hypocritical self-concern betray the ungodly (i.e., compassionless) agenda of the one offering them.
>
> 2.2   Prayers marked by misplaced blame betray the ungodly (i.e., compassionless) agenda of the one offering them.
>
> 2.3   Prayers marked by ostentatious promises betray the ungodly (i.e., compassionless) agenda of the one offering them.
>
> 2.4   Prayers marked by blind prejudices betray the ungodly (i.e., compassionless) agenda of the one offering them.

Theological focus of pericope 2 for preaching

2   The prayers of God's people are consistent with the compassionate character of the God they are called to reflect to others.

Applicational command of pericope 2

2   Pray *with* God![3]

---

3. For specific application that was given to the people of OBC, see the manuscript of this sermon in Appendix B.

PERICOPE 3

Reflecting God's Compassion . . . Indiscriminately (Jonah 3)

[God re-commissions Jonah; Nineveh's repentance; God's mercy]

Theological focus of pericope 3

3   God's people consistently reflect God's own unwavering desire to demonstrate his compassionate character to others regardless of their perceived depth of sin, their ethnicity, or their social status (3:1–10).

3.1   God's people often fail to rightly reflect God's compassionate heart toward others, particularly the "evil" and the "outsider."

3.2   While his people may fail to adequately reflect his character, God unwaveringly longs to demonstrate his compassionate character to all people.

3.3   God's compassion is not limited by perceived levels of sinfulness, national identity, or individual social status.

Theological focus of pericope 3 for preaching

3   God's people indiscriminately reflect God's desire to demonstrate his compassionate character to others regardless of their perceived worthiness.

Applicational command of pericope 3

3   Love across all lines![4]

---

4. For specific application that was given to the people of OBC, see the manuscript of this sermon in Appendix B.

PERICOPE 4

Reflecting God's Compassion . . . Submissively (Jonah 4)

[Jonah's anger with God; God's object lesson for Jonah]

Theological focus of pericope 4

4   Understanding and submitting to God's desire at the expense of their own, God's people reflect his compassionate character to those around them (4:1–11).

     4.1   After understanding God's revealed desire—a desire that is consistent with his character—God's people are to submit to it at the expense of their own.

     4.2   In submitting to God's revealed desire, God's people are to reflect his compassionate character to those around them.

Theological focus of pericope 4 for preaching

4   The people of God reflect the compassionate character of the God who has called them by understanding and submitting to his will at the expense of their own.

Applicational command of pericope 4

4   Love 'til it hurts![5]

---

5. For specific application that was given to the people of OBC, see the manuscript of this sermon in Appendix B.

Appendix B

Sermon Maps and Manuscripts for the Four Pericopes of Jonah

THE FOLLOWING PAGES PROVIDE the mapping of the four pericopes of the book of Jonah. These are equivalent to traditional sermon outlines but focus more on the movements of the text rather than "points." The maps were developed out of the theological foci of their respective pericopes (restated at the top of each map), the major movements being associated with part of that focus stated in Appendix A. After the maps were finalized, sermon manuscripts were developed to be used in the preaching moment.

REFLECTING GOD'S COMPASSION
... OBEDIENTLY (JONAH 1)

Sermon Map

Theological Focus
God's people obediently reflect his compassionate character to those around them and, in so doing, avoid descending from, not his presence but, his blessings.

Introduction

[Image] My sons disobediently riding their bikes to their own harm

[Need] Sometimes God allows his children to experience the consequences of their disobedience to him

[Topic] What does that look like and how can we avoid it?

[Reference] Starting this morning we are going to study a well-known (perhaps one of the most well-known) stories in the Bible—that of Jonah—and we're going to find an example of just that. Jonah disobeys the Lord and is then allowed to experience the consequences of that rebellion. So, this prophet ends up serving as a negative example to us and a reminder as to what's at stake when God calls you and I to obey his voice.

[Organization] Today in chapter 1 we're going to see the disobedience of Jonah, what Jonah desired in that disobedience, and then what actually came of his disobedience.

Body

[Entry signpost] The book famously begins with . . .

I. The disobedience of Jonah

    A. Jonah disobeyed the word of the Lord

        1. Jonah's intentional and sustained flight of disobedience (vv. 1–3).

        2. Jonah's disobedience highlighted via contrast to pagan sailors (vv. 4–16).

B. Relevance: Ways we are tempted to disobey God's word.

[Illustration] A day in the life of potentially disobedient Josiah Boyd

[Transition] Jonah's disobedience didn't accomplish what he wanted it to accomplish.

II. The desired result of his disobedience

    A. Disobedience to the word of the Lord does not remove us from his presence.

        1. Jonah fled with purpose: To get away from the presence of God (vv. 3 [x2], 10).

        2. In spite of Jonah's efforts, God's presence was constant (vv. 4–17).

    B. Relevance: Times we may try to run/hide from God. (Also, times we may feel he's absent.)

    [Illustration] Isaac Watts, "Surrounded"

[Transition] Jonah, a prophet, wasn't thinking rightly about his God. He disobeyed thinking he could get away from the presence of the Lord, but that proved futile. Instead, he experienced something else.

III. The actual result of his disobedience

    A. Disobedience to the word of the Lord removes us from his blessings.

        1. Jonah surrendered the blessing of being used by God (vv. 1–2).

        2. Jonah surrendered the blessing of safety—his and others (vv. 4, 8, 12 et al.).

        3. Jonah surrendered the blessing of a faithful witness (vv. 6, 9, etc.).

    B. Relevance: Do we know all that we give up when we walk in disobedience?

    [Illustration] Jesus Christ (Phil 2:8) as a positive example

[Transition] Jonah didn't do what he should have. God wants us to do better.

IV. *Obey and enjoy!*

    • Identify one thing you feel God is calling you to do

    • "Help me" be obedient; "Thank you" for the blessings to come

Sermon Manuscript

The other day I was watching my two oldest boys ride their bikes in front of our house. As I watched, a game developed in which the younger was determined to not only *catch* his brother on his bike but *hit* his brother with his bike . . . while both were still moving at full speed. Recognizing the many ways that game could not end well—probably from experience—I called out to them, "Stop doing that, you're going to get hurt!"

He obeyed . . . for a minute. But soon "the call of the wild" lured him back into the same risky, and now disobedient, game of bicycle bumper-car tag.

In these moments, anyone who has ever cared for children, has a choice to make. Assessing the potential harm, do you correct the disobedience, or do you allow them to experience the consequences of their disobedience?

The Bible tells us that God parents his children in a similar way. He has been clear in his parental instruction, inviting us to enjoy the abundant life he offers and warning us against activities that will rob us of it. And when we disobey—and we *do* disobey, don't we?—there are times he wisely and lovingly allows us to experience the consequences of our disobedience.

As we begin our study of the book of Jonah, we find an example of just that. Jonah disobeys the Lord and is then allowed to experience the consequences of that rebellion. So, this prophet ends up serving as a negative example to us and a reminder of what is at stake when God calls you and me to obey his voice.

The book famously begins with *the disobedience of Jonah.*

"The word of the Lord came to Jonah the son of Amittai saying, 'Arise, go to Nineveh'" (vv. 1–2a).

Jonah, son of Amittai, was a *real* prophet whose ministry is alluded to in 2 Kings 14. There, as was typical for prophets, he is recorded as bringing God's word to *God's* people, *Israel.* Well, Nineveh is *not* Israel. In fact, it was a city in Assyria which had been, and would be again, an *enemy* of Israel. And, as we continue reading verse 2, we see they really were the bad guys.

"Arise, go to Nineveh the great city and cry against it, for their wickedness has come up before Me" (v. 2).

The imagery is that of evil being piled so high it eventually comes before God's face in heaven. This important Assyrian city, Nineveh, was utterly depraved and their wickedness had reached a critical point, but instead of immediately delivering judgement as would have been the prerogative of a holy and just God, the Lord shows his compassion by taking time to send them a message through his prophet. At least, that's what he's intending to do.

However, that extension of gracious compassion is immediately met with disobedience: "But Jonah rose up to flee to Tarshish from the presence of the Lord" (v. 3a).

For the original audience, these few verses are a shocking opening. Not only has God sent a prophet to Israel's enemies but that same prophet disobeys God and runs in the exact opposite direction as far away as he possibly can. His disobedience is extreme.

It is also intentional: "So he went down to Joppa, found a ship which was going to Tarshish, paid the fare and went down into it to go with them to Tarshish from the presence of the Lord" (v. 3b–c).

Not only has Jonah decided to disobey God, but he's also willing to spend time, energy, and money to do it. Whereas God is being extremely and deliberately compassionate, his prophet is being extremely and deliberately calloused.

And Jonah's lack of compassion, his ungodliness, his callousness—all are highlighted throughout the rest of the chapter by way of contrast to the pagan sailors he encounters on that Tarshish-bound ship.

"The Lord hurled a great wind on the sea and there was a great storm on the sea so that the ship was about to break up. Then the sailors became afraid and every man cried to his god, and they threw the cargo which was in the ship into the sea to lighten it for them. But Jonah had gone below into the hold of the ship, lain down and fallen sound asleep" (vv. 4–5).

These are seasoned boatman—career mariners. They know storms enough to know the severity of *this* one is supernatural. In other words, this is no normal tempest. So, what do they do? Verse 5 says "every man cried to his god." In contrast, where's Jonah? He's doing the most passive and indifferent thing he could do: He's sleeping.

"So the captain approached him and said, 'How is it that you are sleeping? Get up, call on your god. Perhaps your god will be concerned about us so that we will not perish'" (v. 6).

The captain finds Jonah, wakes him, and tells him to join them in begging the gods for mercy. One of the deities must be responsible; perhaps it's this stowaway's God—the other ones don't seem to be listening.

"Each man said to his mate, 'Come, let us cast lots so we may learn on whose account this calamity has struck us.' So they cast lots and the lot fell on Jonah. Then they said to him, 'Tell us, now! On whose account has this calamity struck us? What is your occupation? And where do you come from? What is your country? From what people are you'" (vv. 7–8)?

Desperate to find the object of the god's anger, the men turn to a game of chance, but we know there's no chance involved in the answer they get.

With all signs pointing to Jonah, they interrogate him and eventually pry a confession out of the runaway prophet in verse 9.

Now, as I read his confession, notice that up until this point the sailors had been beseeching generic "gods," but here Jonah drops the covenant name of Israel's "Lord God"—*Yahweh Elohim.*

"He said to them, 'I am a Hebrew, and I fear the Lord God of heaven who made the sea and the dry land'" (v. 9).

In other words: "The God I serve, the Lord God, created that which is about to kill us ('the sea') and that to which we long to see again ('the dry land'). My God not only runs them and owns them but created them."

It's quite a reverent statement from this unfaithful prophet, isn't it? While Jonah may be running from God, he knows well the God he's running from. He's not fleeing in ignorance. He's well-aware of Who it is he's disobeying. The rebel has good theology.

How do the sailors respond to Jonah's declaration?

"Then the men became extremely frightened and they said to him, 'How could you do this?' For the men knew that he was fleeing from the presence of the Lord, because he had told them" (v. 10).

The sailors are confused as to how someone can believe what he believes about his God and still run from that same God, a God obviously far more powerful than any of the gods they've ever known.

They ask Jonah what can be done to appease *Yahweh Elohim*, the God of the Hebrews, the God of the heavens, the God who made the sea and the dry land. From this point on there is no more mention of generic "gods," but only *the* Lord God.

"So they said to him, 'What should we do to you that the sea may become calm for us?'—for the sea was becoming increasingly stormy. He said to them, 'Pick me up and throw me into the sea. Then the sea will become calm for you, for I know that on account of me this great storm has come upon you'" (vv. 11–12).

Instead of repenting of his disobedience or telling the sailors to take him back to land so he can fulfill his assignment, Jonah would rather die. It is clear God won't let him run away but that doesn't mean he has to obey. He'll take death at sea over obedience, but he won't do it himself. Instead, he asks for sailor-assisted suicide, not because he wants to save their lives but because he doesn't want to save Nineveh.

"However, the men rowed desperately to return to land, but they could not, for the sea was becoming even stormier against them" (v. 13).

The sailors now know that throwing this stranger—a stranger who has endangered their lives and livelihoods—into the water will save their lives, yet they try everything they can to *not* do that. The pagan sailors show compassion for the well-being of a rebel—exactly what Jonah was supposed to do at the beginning of the book but didn't.

The irony here is thick. God, a compassionate God, wanted his servant, Jonah, to show that same compassion to the wayward Nineveh. Instead, we have godless, pantheistic sailors showing God's compassion. They're looking more like Yahweh than Yahweh's prophet!

"Then they called on the Lord and said, 'We earnestly pray, O Lord, do not let us perish on account of this man's life and do not put innocent blood on us; for You, O Lord, have done as You have pleased.' So they picked up Jonah, threw him into the sea, and the sea stopped its raging" (vv. 14–15).

With God stripping away every other option they had, the sailors reverently call out to *Yahweh Elohim* for mercy and then reluctantly toss Jonah overboard, and the sea goes to glass.

"Then the men feared the Lord greatly, and they offered a sacrifice to the Lord and made vows" (v. 16).

The sailors didn't know a lot about *Yahweh Elohim*, the God of the Hebrews, the God of the Bible, the one true living God. But what they did now know moved them to awe and adoration. They knew enough to be moved to action.

Jonah, on the other hand, knew God well, yet his stubborn disobedience found him sinking to the bottom of the sea.

The chapter closes as it opened: with God's compassion on display. "And the Lord appointed a great fish to swallow Jonah, and Jonah was in the stomach of the fish three days and three nights" (v. 17).

Just like God could have destroyed evil Nineveh, so too God could have let rebellious Jonah die. But, in both cases, he determines to send help.

The word of the Lord came to Jonah son of Amittai, and Jonah disobeyed the word of the Lord.

Whenever I read this chapter, I find myself shaking my head at Jonah in condescending disapproval until I remember how easy it is to replace Jonah's name with mine in that sentence: The word of the Lord came to Josiah son of George, and Josiah disobeyed the word of the Lord.

As clear a directive as "Arise, go to Nineveh" is, so too is "In your anger, do not sin," "Do not let any unwholesome talk come out of your mouths," "Honor your father and mother," "Do everything without grumbling or arguing," "Rejoice in the Lord always," and "Devote yourselves to prayer."

And the word of the Lord came to Josiah. Does he obey or run away? And the word of the Lord came to you. Did you obey or run away?

Years ago, I was pulled over for speeding. It was cottage season, and the highway was busy, and when the officer came to my window, I pointed out that I hadn't been going any faster than anyone else. The officer said, "That's nice. Here's your ticket." I could complicate the issue by trying to justify my actions, but the bottom line was that I had disobeyed the speed limit.

If we're honest, most of the time obedience is not that complicated. We confuse it with rationalizations and justifications but much of the time it's pretty simple.

Jonah disobeyed God. Period. But he didn't do so without a reason. In fact, the text makes clear *the desired result of his disobedience,* that is, what he was trying to accomplish by fleeing.

"But Jonah rose up to flee to Tarshish *from the presence of the Lord.* So he went down to Joppa, found a ship which was going to Tarshish, paid the fare and went down into it to go with them to Tarshish *from the presence of the Lord. . . .* Then the men became extremely frightened and they said to him, 'How could you do this?' For the men knew that he was fleeing *from the presence of the Lord,* because he had told them" (vv. 3, 10).

Why did Jonah run? What was the desired result of his disobedience? He wanted to get away from the Lord. Jonah wanted to remove himself from God's service, God's will, and God reign. He wanted to get away from the presence of God.

But he couldn't do it, could he? In spite of his efforts to flee God's presence, God's presence was constant throughout the chapter. It was on display in the storm that he: hurled upon the sea (v. 4), made worse (vv. 11, 13), and then stopped altogether (v. 15). God was present in the storm.

God's presence was on display when the fearful sailors cast lots to determine who had angered the gods and the lots "just-so-happened" to fall on Jonah. God was present in the lots.

God's presence was on display as the great fish came upon the sinking Hebrew and spared his life.

The desired result of Jonah's disobedience was unobtainable. What he desired most—to be away from the presence of God—he could not have.

And neither can we. The God of the Bible is fully present everywhere always.

"'Can a man hide himself in hiding places so I do not see him?' declares the Lord. 'Do I not fill the heavens and the earth?' declares the Lord" (Jer 23:24).

"Where can I go from Your Spirit? Or where can I flee from Your presence? If I ascend to heaven, You are there; If I make my bed in Sheol, behold, You are there. If I take the wings of the dawn, If I dwell in the remotest part of the sea, Even there Your hand will lead me, And Your right hand will lay hold of me" (Ps 139:7–10).

The God of the Bible is fully present everywhere always.

If we are living in disobedience and lying to ourselves like Jonah, thinking we can out-run and out-maneuver God, the reality of his omnipresence should be haunting. He is everywhere!

But if we are walking in obedience, it's life-giving. In times when we feel alone, scared, vulnerable, helpless, the reality of his omnipresence offers comfort and peace. He is everywhere!

Isaac Watts, in his hymn entitled *Lord, Thou Hast Planted With Thy Hands* wrote: "Within thy circling power I stand / On every side I find thy hand / Awake, asleep, at home, abroad, / I am surrounded still with God."

Jonah disobeyed God's word and the text reveals the desired result of that rebellion, a result that was impossible. So, what was *the actual result of his disobedience*? To say it another way, what were the consequences of his disobedience that God allowed Jonah to experience?

We see in this passage that, while his disobedience didn't remove Jonah from God's presence like he wanted, it *did* remove him from God's blessings. Let me quickly point out three such blessings that Jonah forfeited because of his rebellion. These are consequences of his disobedience.

First, Jonah surrendered the blessing of being used by God. In the opening two verses Jonah is invited to be an extension of God's compassion to the Ninevites. But by running the opposite direction, he forfeited that privilege.

Second, Jonah surrendered the blessing of safety. Now, obedience to God doesn't guarantee physical safety, but in the case of Jonah, his disobedience brought disciplinary and corrective danger. And the poor sailors were caught in the crossfire! Because of Jonah's rebellion, not only was his safety in question, but so was the safety of those around him.

Third, Jonah surrendered the blessing of being a faithful witness. While he had forfeited the privilege of being God's mouthpiece to Nineveh, God graciously gave him an audience with the pagan sailors. But Jonah was so cemented in his rebellion that he failed to represent God well even in that circumstance. He gave up the blessing of being a faithful witness for his God.

While the *desired* result of his disobedience was his removal from God's presence, the *actual* result of his disobedience was his removal from God's blessings—blessings of being used by God, of safety for himself and those around him, and of being a faithful witness.

Disobedience is never free. Do we even realize all we give up when we rebel against our Heavenly Father? Do we understand all we forfeit? Peace? Assurance? Joy? Future rewards? Yes. Yes. Yes. Yes.

What about the ability to be a faithful witness for him in this world and to those God has placed around us?

What about safety? Passages like 1 Corinthians 11:30 and Acts 5 make it clear that disobedience to the Lord *can* bring about physical illness as discipline and correction, for us and those around us.

What about the blessing of being used by God? In Revelation 3, Christ is speaking to a group of believers who allowed themselves to become apathetic and useless for his work, and he says, "I will spit you out of my mouth!" In other words, "Your aversion and apathy to being useful to God is disgusting!"

You see, like Jonah, when we disobey God and run from opportunities to demonstrate his compassionate character to others, we are never removing ourselves from his presence, but we are removing ourselves from his blessings, blessings he longs to bestow upon us but which we sacrifice in our rebellion.

And so, through Jonah chapter 1, God's people are being reminded and called to *obey and enjoy!* Obey the word of the Lord and then enjoy the blessings that he desires to shower upon us, not the least of which is the privilege of being conduits of God's compassionate character to those around us. Obey and enjoy!

In the hours following this message, I want to encourage you to try this: Type into a search engine on your phone or computer something like "New Testament imperatives" or "New Testament commands." You'll find a huge list, but we'll narrow it down. Scan through that list and find one that comes from an epistle, a letter like Ephesians, Philippians, or Colossians. Narrowing the search this way not only makes the list manageable but also ensures easy applicability for us today as those letters were written specifically to post-Pentecost believers like us.

Now, pick one that strikes you as particularly and personally difficult. One that you know you need to learn to obey.

For example: "Speak truth . . . to your neighbor" (Eph 4:25). "Children, obey your parents" (6:1). "Let your gentle spirit be known to all" (Phil 4:5). "Set your mind on things above" (Col 3:2).

Once you've selected one command, write the reference of that command in your Bible next to Jonah 1 and pray two things as you look at that reference: "Help me" and "thank you." Help me God, be obedient to this command, and thank you for the blessings to come.

The word of the Lord came to Jonah, and Jonah disobeyed the word of the Lord. In so doing, he didn't remove himself from God's presence like he wanted, but he did remove himself from God's blessings, particularly the blessing of being used by God as a conduit, an agent, of God's compassionate character to those around him.

We can, and must, learn from the example of the wayward prophet. Brothers and sisters, we can, by the power of God, obey God. And we will, by the grace of God, enjoy his promised blessings. *Obey and enjoy!*

REFLECTING GOD'S COMPASSION
. . . CONSISTENTLY (JONAH 2)

Sermon Map

Theological Focus
The prayers of God's people are consistent with the compassionate
character of the God they are called to reflect to others.

Introduction

[Image] The rarity of seeing someone's heart with clarity—i.e., windows
into the soul (e.g., a diary, a child's letter to Santa, how the church
sings, prayer)

[Need] The prayers we offer to God—as individuals, families, and as a
church family—can reveal what we truly believe about God, ourselves, and the task we've been entrusted with by him in this world.

[Topic] Can you imagine if someone was eavesdropping and recording all
of your times of prayer with God? After you recover from the hor-
ror of even that thought, what do you suppose they would learn
about you from listening?

[Reference] In the second chapter of Jonah, we're given an inspired eavesdropping session on the now all-wet prophet. And it's quite telling.

[Organization] What we're going to find is a prayer of self-preservation
and of self-righteousness and notice the dramatic contrast that it is
to the God who sent Jonah to Nineveh in the first place, a God of
generosity, patience, and compassion.

Body

[Introduction to tone] Some read this psalm as genuine repentance by the
prophet. However, in addition to the textual clues that we're going
to look at in a moment as we walk through the chapter, there are
some issues of trajectory when we look at the whole book that make
me think even his prayer is marked by hypocrisy, irony, and sin.

[Entry signpost] The psalm opens with Jonah calling out to God, for the first time, in desperation.

I. A prayer of self-preservation

    A. While offered to a God of life-giving compassion, Jonah's prayer is marked only by self-preservation (vv. 1–6b).

        1. Jonah breaks the silence (vv. 1–2)

        2. Jonah blames his God (vv. 3–4)

        3. Jonah bemoans his situation (vv. 5–6b)

        4. (Any acknowledgement of guilt, sin, or disobedience?)

    B. Relevance: When do we talk to God? Do we only call out to our compassionate God when we've come to the end of our abilities? Are our prayers merely those of self-preservation?

    [Illustration] Relationships of convenience; "fox-hole" prayers

[Transition] While the first half of the psalm betrays the motive of self-preservation, the latter half reveals something even more troubling.

II. A prayer of self-righteousness

    A. While offered to a God of others-focused compassion, Jonah's prayer is marked only by self-righteousness (vv. 6c–10).

        1. "God, I'm worth saving" (vv. 4b, 6c).

        2. "God, I'm worth hearing" (v. 7).

        3. "God, I'm worth seeing" (vv. 8–9).

    B. Relevance: Do we pray in humble dependance? Are our prayers, though perhaps full of orthodox understandings of God, marked by self-righteousness?

    [Illustration] Luke 18:9–14

[Transition] How can we learn, once again, from Jonah's bad example?

III. *Pray* with *God!*

    • Ask the Spirit to empower you and the Scriptures to guide you (e.g., Lord's Prayer).

    • If our prayers are windows into our souls, we want them to reflect a heart that is consistent with the character of the God to whom we pray.

Sermon Manuscript

In the early twentieth century, artist Blanche Lazzell wrote this in her diary: "This book is not intended for other eyes than the writer's, and when they are forever closed, I hope this book will be laid in the fire."[1]

Lazzell later became a well-known artist and, despite her wishes for privacy, her diary is now part of a permanent collection in the Smithsonian Archives, on display for all to see and read.

Why is that a horrifying thought for diary-keepers everywhere? Why does the idea of a stranger reading your journal make you uncomfortable?

Could it be because a journal or diary is where the desperately private becomes potentially public? It's a place many go to be totally vulnerable, unreserved, and exposed. In many ways, it's a window into the true self: the depravity, imperfection, and insecurity that's otherwise skillfully kept hidden. To have all of that and more laid bare is unnerving.

The Christian prayer life is like a diary. In prayer we can express our deepest sorrows, greatest triumphs, embarrassing blunders, and darkest rage. In prayer we confess sin, admit insufficiency, and ask forgiveness.

Like reading someone's diary can give you "a window into their soul," so to speak, so too can listening to the prayers of a person, a family, or a church family. *How* we pray, *when* we pray, and *what* we pray for often reveals what we truly believe about God, ourselves, and life in a fallen world.

Can you imagine if someone was eavesdropping and recording all of your prayers? *Shudder* If that was the case, though, what would they learn about you?

In the second chapter of Jonah, we're given an inspired eavesdropping session on the prayers of the prophet. And by listening in we learn a lot about him.

What we're going to find is a hypocritical prayer marked by self-preservation, self-exoneration, and self-righteousness, characteristics that are especially disagreeable when contrasted with the character of the God to whom the prayers are being directed, a God who is generous, patient, and compassionate.

This prayer gives us a look into Jonah's heart and invites you and me to examine our own.

Before we get to the prayer, let's remind ourselves of where we are in the story. In chapter 1, the Lord gives his prophet, Jonah, a surprising assignment, one that showcased God's compassionate character. Jonah disobeyed

---

1. Accessed September 2020 from https://www.smithsonianmag.com/smithsonian -institution/peering-secret-diaries-american-artists-180952879/

God, running in the opposite direction trying to remove himself from the Lord's presence.

This is, obviously, a futile task, and God proved inescapable, hurling a great storm upon the ship—Jonah's chosen escape vehicle. The sailors eventually learn it is Jonah's disobedience putting their lives in danger and ask him, "What can we do to make it stop?" He answers, "Throw me into the sea."

The pagan sailors—behaving more like God than God's prophet—try everything they can not to kill Jonah, but in the end they have no choice. And when the prophet's body hits the water, the storm ceases, Jonah sinks, and the ship sails on. But, instead of letting him die like he deserves, God once again demonstrates his compassion by sending a great fish to swallow and deliver his prophet.

Now we come to chapter 2 and the exposing entry into Jonah's diary of prayer. The prayer is bracketed by verses 1 and 10 which transition out of and back into the narrative. Verses 2 through 9, the prayer proper, is recorded in the form of a thanksgiving psalm, which really adds to the irony because the content doesn't match the form. Instead of worshipful gratitude, we find selfishness, entitlement, and pride. As I said, prayers can reveal the heart of the pray-er.

The psalm begins with Jonah calling out in desperation with the only goal being *self-preservation*.

"From inside the fish Jonah prayed to the Lord his God. He said: 'In my distress I called to the Lord, and he answered me. From deep in the realm of the dead I called for help, and you listened to my cry'" (vv. 1–2).

This is the first time Jonah has spoken to God in this book. He didn't address God in his confusion regarding his assignment. He didn't voice his disagreement. He didn't request understanding. He didn't even ask for God to spare the lives of the sailors as they fought against the storm he caused. No. The first time we have Jonah, the prophet *of* God, speaking *to* God, is when he's sinking to the bottom of the sea.

He was about to drown, and it's in that "distress" that he called out to the Lord; "from deep in the realm of the dead" he "called for help." And, once again highlighting the compassionate character of the God from whom he had run and to whom he was now speaking, the Lord "answered" and "listened to" his rebellious prophet by sending the great fish.

Again, we're confronted with the contrast between the patient and compassionate God and the haughty and self-centered prophet. It's revealing that Jonah only calls out to God when his back is against the wall.

These back-against-the-wall requests to God are sometimes called "foxhole prayers," so named for soldiers pinned down in a bunker, surrounded by enemies. In those moments, soldiers may call out to God as a last resort.

I've prayed those prayers in desperate times. I'm sure you have also. David, in the Psalms, prayed out of helplessness. Jesus, with the cross looming, called out to the Father in prayer. I believe God wants us calling upon him in our times of greatest need. There's nothing wrong with foxhole prayers, except perhaps when they're our *only* prayers.

It's as a last resort that Jonah calls out to God from his watery foxhole. It's all about self-preservation. Even worse, in the next two verses Jonah actually blames *God* for the foxhole! He moves from self-preservation to self-exoneration:

"*You* hurled me into the depths, into the very heart of the seas, and the currents swirled about me; all *your* waves and breakers swept over me. I said, 'I have been banished from your sight'" (vv. 3–4b).

Who hurled Jonah into the sea? Technically, the sailors, because Jonah wouldn't do it himself. But the prophet points the finger at God. "You did this. You may have used a storm and sailors, but it's on you, God. They are '*your* waves and breakers' that 'swept over me.' You cast me aside."

We're all invited to Jonah's pity-party in verse 4 as he laments being "banished from" God's sight.

Hang on a minute! Think back to chapter 1: Wasn't it Jonah's desire to get away from the presence of God? Wasn't that the thrice-stated reason he disobeyed? It was! And now he's blaming God for the apparent realization of the goal. "I'm passive in this whole thing! I'm a victim! 'I've been banished from your sight!'" That's revisionist history. He's experiencing what he longed for, doesn't like it, and now he's blaming God and exonerating himself. "It's not my fault!"

The pity-party continues: "The engulfing waters threatened me, the deep surrounded me; seaweed was wrapped around my head. To the roots of the mountains I sank down; the earth beneath barred me in forever" (vv. 5–6b).

Such strong language used to describe the hopelessness of his circumstances. He was trapped, approaching death, helpless, and powerless.

Now, at this point let's pause and ask a very important question: Has there been *any* acknowledgement of guilt, sin, or disobedience on the part of Jonah? None! Nothing even close to resembling repentance.

What we have instead is a woe-is-me description of his troubles, troubles that, while self-inflicted, he blames on the One who has just delivered him. This is nothing more than a stilted prayer of self-preservation and self-exoneration. And, like a diary in a museum exhibit, it reveals to all who read it the heart of this prophet.

Just as I've prayed prayers of self-preservation, I've prayed prayers of self-exoneration; prayers in which I try to justify my sin to the God who sees all and who has delivered me from the bondage and power of that sin.

"God, if you hadn't made me the way you made me . . .; If you hadn't brought that person into my life . . .; God, you gave me the family I have . . . You failed to give me the strength . . . You aren't clear in your expectations . . . You're not helping me enough . . . You hurled me into the depths! These are your waves and breakers!" That's self-exoneration. That's praying like Jonah, unrepentantly shifting the blame to the One who has provided salvation. Maybe you can relate.

As we've seen, Jonah's prayer in chapter 2 has been motivated by self-preservation and stained by self-exoneration. In what's left we're going to find what may be the worst yet: Self-righteousness.

It becomes clear that Jonah believes he's worthy to be saved by God, worthy to be heard by God, and worthy to be seen by God. His prayer is soaked in self-righteousness.

Scan back to verse 4: "Yet I will look again toward your holy temple" (v. 4c–d).

Do you hear the presumption? "God, I'm worth saving!"

You might say, *Hey, Jonah's just calling out in faith!* Maybe. But I think the rest of the clues point toward hypocrisy, not humility.

Drop to verse 6: "But you, Lord my God, brought my life up from the pit" (v. 6c–d).

Of course, he did! Because Jonah is worthy of salvation, isn't he? God already saved Jonah from drowning by way of the fish and now, sitting inside his fishy ark of deliverance, Jonah boldly claims his certainty of total restoration. "I will again walk into the temple. There's no doubt. God will restore me." This is Jonah self-righteously declaring: "God, I'm worth saving!"

"When my life was ebbing away, I remembered you, Lord, and my prayer rose to you, to your holy temple" (v. 7).

While he believes he's worth saving, Jonah now self-righteously declares: "God, I'm worth hearing!" My prayer rose to you, right into your holy temple. I spoke and my requests came before you. All Jonah had to do to have God's ear, apparently, was "remember" him—to bring to mind the God he had been ignoring, running from, disobeying, misrepresenting, and rebelling against. But even though he hasn't spoken to him throughout, all he does is bring him to mind and his prayers of desperation zip right up to God's ear; they rise before God.

Interestingly, the last thing said to have risen before the Lord's face was the wickedness of Nineveh (1:2). Coincidence?

It is a privilege to be heard by God. It is a miracle of divine provision that the Creator of all things bends his ear to the calls from his creatures. Jonah, as disobedient and rebellious as he had been, takes it for granted: "He'll hear me. I'm worth hearing."

Finally: "Those who cling to worthless idols turn away from God's love for them. But I, with shouts of grateful praise, will sacrifice to you. What I have vowed I will make good. I will say, 'Salvation comes from the Lord'" (vv. 8–9).

Here's where the self-righteousness really comes to a head. Who do you think Jonah is referring to when he says, in verse 8, "those who cling to worthless idols turn away from God's love for them"? Or it could be translated: "those who cling to empty faiths reject God's extended mercy." Who in this story are holding tightly to idolatry and, in so doing, rejecting the compassionate love God longs to extend to them?

I think it's Nineveh! They were the godless people to whom Jonah was originally sent. Jonah, in these two final lines of his prayer, is bringing it back full circle to his assignment and comparing himself with the Ninevites, those evil, wicked, undeserving monsters.

Those sinners over there, those God-haters, they cling so tightly to their false gods they don't deserve the love and compassion of the true God.

And then the all-revealing first two words of verse 9: "But I." Those sinners don't deserve to be in the presence of a compassionate and loving God, but I, I will be in your presence. I will come before you in praise that you'll no doubt accept and rejoice in. I will make sacrifices to you that you'll love and make vows to you that you'll gush over.

In his self-righteousness, Jonah has already claimed "God, I'm worth saving" and "God, I'm worth hearing" but here he adds to the list "God, I'm worth seeing." Not like those dirty Assyrian sinners. I'm your guy. "Salvation comes from the Lord" but only to those worthy like me, only to those worthy like Israel.

I've prayed in self-preservation and with self-exoneration. And, if I'm honest, I've prayed prayers stained with self-righteousness as well. I've taken for granted the privilege of having the ear of my Creator and Sustainer. I've allowed thoughts of my own worthiness to creep into how I speak about others. "Those people over there, they kind of deserve what they're getting. Having been delivered from death through faith in Christ, I, obviously, deserve something better."

I love the parable Jesus told in Luke 18.

"To some who were confident of their own righteousness and looked down on everyone else, Jesus told this parable:

"'Two men went up to the temple to pray, one a Pharisee and the other a tax collector. The Pharisee stood by himself and prayed: 'God, I thank you that I am not like other people—robbers, evildoers, adulterers—or even like this tax collector. I fast twice a week and give a tenth of all I get.'

"'But the tax collector stood at a distance. He would not even look up to heaven, but beat his breast and said, 'God, have mercy on me, a sinner.'

"'I tell you that this man, rather than the other, went home justified before God. For all those who exalt themselves will be humbled, and those who humble themselves will be exalted'" (Luke 18:9–14).

Was Jonah the pharisee in this story or the tax collector? Which am I? Which are you?

Jonah's prayer was motivated by self-preservation, marked by self-exoneration, and stained with self-righteousness. It's little wonder, having to listen to it, the fish threw up.

"And the Lord commanded the fish, and it vomited Jonah onto dry land" (v. 10).

Just as Lazzell's diary was an exposing look into the artist's heart, so too was Jonah's prayer. It revealed what was going on internally; what he thought about God, about himself, and about his assignment in the world.

The same is true with our prayers. What do they reveal about us?

Through the negative example of Jonah in this "psalm of thanksgiving," we are being invited to *Pray with God! To pray with God!* To shape our prayers in such a way as they reflect the compassionate character of the God to whom we're praying. We're to *Pray with God!*

Jonah, in many ways, was *praying* against God in chapter 2 just as he had been *running* against God in chapter 1. God is compassionate and loving and longs for people to come to him in faith. Jonah didn't share that sentiment nor that godly character, and his prayers reflected that. You and I need to *Pray with God!* not against him.

Practically speaking, this means asking the Holy Spirit to *empower* you in prayer and allowing the Scriptures to *guide* you in prayer.

One way we can be sure we're praying with God is to pray his words back to him. Think about it. When we use the Bible to shape our prayers, we are literally quoting God's infallible word back to him.

And there are many prayers in the Bible to use as guides. In fact, there's a 150-chapter book full of them called the Psalms. But there are many others sprinkled throughout its inerrant pages as well.

In fact, in my Bible I have every prayer marked in the margin with a "P" so that I can more easily find them and use them to shape my prayers. When it comes to prayer, who better to learn from than the inspired authors of Scripture, right?

You see, like a secret diary, our hearts are revealed in how we pray. But, at the same time, how we pray shapes our hearts. Back and forth it goes and it can be a beautiful upward spiral of spiritual maturity.

I encourage you, this week, to find a biblical prayer, maybe even the Lord's Prayer in Matthew 6, and use it to help you begin to learn to—and continue to—*Pray with God!*

REFLECTING GOD'S COMPASSION . . . INDISCRIMINATELY (JONAH 3)

Sermon Map

Theological Focus

God's people indiscriminately reflect God's desire to demonstrate his compassionate character to others regardless of their perceived worthiness.

Introduction

[Image] James 1:22–25, mirror for ourselves in the word

[Need] Looking into a mirror isn't always enjoyable, is it? Sometimes we don't like all we see. But it's healthy, especially when that mirror is Scripture, our guide is the Holy Spirit, and the goal is Christlikeness.

[Topic] So let's look together into the mirror again this morning.

[Reference] Please turn, if you haven't already, to Jonah 3. As you turn, let's remember that the prophet has just been vomited up onto dry land by the great fish that God sent to save his life and he's immediately met with a familiar command.

[Organization] First we're going to see Jonah's heart for "the outsider" and then we'll see God's heart for "the outsider." And as the book contrasts the two for us, we're invited then to examine our own hearts.

Body

[Entry signpost] First, let's consider what the text reveals about . . .

I. Jonah's heart for "the outsider"

    A. God's people often fail to rightly reflect God's compassionate heart toward others, particularly the "evil" and the "outsider"

        1. Looking *back* to understand Jonah's heart (chs. 1, 2)

        2. Looking *at Jonah* to understand Jonah's heart (3:1–4)

        3. Looking *at Nineveh* to understand Jonah's heart (3:5–9)

4. Looking *forward* to understand Jonah's heart (ch. 4)

B. Relevance: Ways we may discriminate in perceived worthiness for the reception of God's grace

[Illustration] People with a specific sin struggle; James 2

[Transition] Now that we've considered Jonah's heart for "the outsider," let's now turn our attention to . . .

II. God's heart for "the outsider"

A. While his people may fail to adequately reflect it, God longs to demonstrate his compassionate character to *all* people, regardless of levels of sinfulness, national identities, or individual social status.

1. Looking *back* to understand God's heart (chs. 1, 2)

2. Looking *around* to understand God's heart (3:10)

B. Relevance: Do we realize that we too were/are "outsiders" to whom God extended his love?

[Illustration] Romans 5:8; James 2:1; 2 Peter 3:9; John 4

[Transition] God's heart's desire is that his compassionate character be made known to all people, regardless of perceived level of sinfulness, nationality, ethnicity, or social status. Jonah failed to grasp this and, thus, failed to reflect this truth. You and I must not. Instead, we are called to . . .

III. *Love across all lines!*

• Pray (for discernment, humility)

• Identify (one "outsider" in your life)

• Connect (with that individual in love)

Sermon Manuscript

In the opening chapter of his New Testament letter, the Apostle James insists that God's word is given, not for mere *information*, but for *application* and life *transformation*.

"Do not merely listen to the word, and so deceive yourselves. Do what it says. Anyone who listens to the word but does not do what it says is like someone who looks at his face in a mirror and, after looking at himself, goes away and immediately forgets what he looks like. But whoever looks intently into the perfect law that gives freedom and continues in it—not forgetting what they have heard but doing it—they will be blessed in what they do" (Jas 1:22–25).

Some look into the mirror of the Bible, rightly see themselves there, but then ignore what they see. These are the *hearers* only. Others look into the mirror, are convicted, and determine to change. These are the *doers*, and they will be blessed.

One author has captured this well: "For me a mirror is not a reflector of reinforcement but a tool of conviction. That's how we use a mirror most effectively, to find where we need to change. The only ones who use a mirror for reinforcement are those who think they need no improvement. God's mirror—the Bible—is not intended for our reaffirmation and reinforcement. God's word is given to us for change."[2]

Over the past couple of weeks, we've been staring into the mirror of the book of Jonah, the over-arching theme of which is that God is a *compassionate* God who wants his people to reflect his compassionate character to the world in which they live.

The prophet Jonah serves as an altogether negative example of this task, providing a picture of what-not-to-do and how-not-to-live.

In chapter 1 we saw a *prodigal* prophet running *from* God. And we looked into that mirror and had to ask ourselves: *Do I reflect God's compassion obediently?*

In chapter 2 we saw a *pious* prophet praying *against* God. And we looked into that mirror again and asked ourselves: *Do I reflect God's compassion consistently?* That is, is my heart consistent with God's heart?

In chapter 3, the text in which we land today, we're going to find Jonah a *pedestrian* prophet speaking *for* God. And we're going to look into that mirror and ask ourselves: *Do I reflect God's compassion indiscriminately?*—that is, without reservation or bias.

---

2. Bailey, *To Follow Him*, 73.

Looking into a mirror isn't always enjoyable, is it? Sometimes we don't like all we see. But it's healthy, especially when that mirror is Scripture, our guide is the Holy Spirit, and the goal is Christlikeness.

So, let's look to the mirror together now. Please turn, if you haven't already, to Jonah 3. As you turn, let's remember that the prophet has just been vomited up onto dry land by the great fish that God sent to save his life and he's immediately met with a familiar command.

"Now the word of the Lord came to Jonah the second time, saying, "Arise, go to Nineveh the great city and proclaim to it the proclamation which I am going to tell you" (vv. 1–2).

The language here is almost identical to that of 1:1–2. This is a recommissioning—a resending. It's as though God says, "Okay, Jonah, let's try this again. Go. To. Nineveh."

And, to the original audience's relief, *this* time the prophet obeys.

"So Jonah arose and went to Nineveh according to the word of the Lord" (v. 3a).

If only he had done that the first time! But, perhaps, better late than never.

Now, as the chapter continues, we're going to find Nineveh taking centerstage. The people, the king, and even the animals of this wicked city become the focus of most of the chapter and the author does that for a very specific reason.

You see, to a Hebrew, who were the Ninevites? They were enemies, pagans, debauched, and sinful. They were, in a word, "outsiders." They were *outside* God's people, *outside* God's blessing, *outside* God's invitation, *outside* God's plan, and *outside* God's purpose. And the Holy Spirit, working through the human author of this book, takes these "outsiders," places them in the middle of the story, to highlight the contrasting reactions to them by God and God's prophet. In other words, in Jonah 3, we are going to be shown, on one side, Jonah's heart for "the outsider" and, on the other side, God's heart for "the outsider." And, seeing them both and comparing them, you and I are then going to be invited to examine our own hearts for "the outsiders" in our lives.

First, let's consider what the text reveals about *Jonah's heart for "the outsider."*

In chapter 1, you'll recall, God told Jonah to go to Nineveh to bring those evil people a message, but Jonah ran away. In fact, as that chapter continued, we learned Jonah would rather die than visit those wicked people. In chapter 2, while thanking God for showing *him* mercy, Jonah declares that "those who cling to empty faith" [like the Ninevites] "forego

God's compassion" (2:8). In other words, they don't deserve God's mercy like Jonah clearly does.

So, judging from chapters 1 and 2, how would we describe the prophet's heart for "the outsider"? Calloused? Indifferent? Vengeful? At the very least we could say he doesn't believe they deserve to witness or experience God's compassion.

In fact, in chapter 4 (spoiler alert!), Jonah admits this is exactly the case. The reason he ran from God in the first place was that he knew God would probably show compassion to those he felt didn't deserve it!

With that in mind, let's go back to verse 3: "So Jonah arose and went to Nineveh according to the word of the Lord. Now Nineveh was an exceedingly great city, a three days' walk" (v. 3).

In addition to a statement of Jonah's long-overdue obedience, we're also given some information about Nineveh. It's a great, important city. Literally, the Hebrew says it "was great to God." So, not only is it great in size (a three-day journey), but it's also important in the eyes of the Lord.

"Then Jonah began to go through the city, one day's walk; and he cried out and said, "Yet forty days and Nineveh will be overthrown" (v. 4).

Finally, the wicked city of Nineveh hears the warning of pending divine judgment. "Judgement is coming!"

Now, we can interpret this verse in one of two ways. Option one: Jonah is doing exactly what he's told. He goes through the city preaching, and his message is so powerful that it only takes one of the three days necessary to have its affect. That's to paint the prophet in the best light possible.

Option two, the one I'm going to suggest, I find more consistent with what we know about Jonah so far and the trajectory of the book as a whole.

I think Jonah, though being obedient, is doing so begrudgingly. Chapter 4 will reveal that he still hates Nineveh and doesn't think they deserve to be spared. So, I read 3:4 describing the prophet as doing the bare minimum— cutting corners on his assignment. I think, though Nineveh is a three-days walk (v. 3), Jonah only does one (v. 4). He pokes his head into the city, does a third of his task. And I also think he delivers a truncated message from God. In Hebrew, Jonah says only five words to the Ninevites. I think, motivated by his disdain for Nineveh, the prophet of God does the absolute bare minimum for them while still being able to say he was obedient to his God.

Imagine a parent tells their teenager to clean their room. Instead, without saying a word, the child storms out of the house and hitchhikes to Mexico to get away from the parent and their "stupid chores." The parent has no choice but to involve the police who apprehend the teen a few days later and bring them back home. The parent now looks at their child and says again, "Clean your room." This time the child, still visibly angry, gets up, walks to their room, and gets to work.

Do you think that child is cleaning *well*? Do you think they're working with joy in their heart? Or do you think there's a chance they may cut corners, stuff a bunch of dirty clothes under their bed just to say they did what the parent asked? In light of previous disobedience, it's a good question.

Now, at dinner that night, a long-overdue conversation finally takes place in which the child blows-up: "I hate cleaning my room, and I'm sick of you trying to get me to do things I don't want to do. I know you well enough to know that you'll just ask me to do it again next week, so what's the point!?"

Now, with that outburst added to the equation, what do you think the chances are that, if that parent goes to inspect the bedroom, they'll find it wasn't really cleaned all that well? Probably pretty high, right? Why? Because it's consistent with what the teenager has shown about their character, their priorities, and their heart.

So too with Jonah here. Knowing what we know about his past rebellion and knowing that a blow-up is coming in chapter 4, it makes sense to me to read 3:4 with suspicion. Jonah's heart for Nineveh hasn't been one of compassion so far, and it won't be in chapter 4 either, so why would it suddenly be in chapter 3?

No, Jonah's heart for "the outsider" is one of indifference at best and hatred at worst. He believes that God's compassion, mercy, and love should be reserved for those who deserve it, people like him, for example, and nations like Israel.

So, Jonah begrudgingly obeys God, and look what happens: "Then the people of Nineveh believed in God; and they called a fast and put on sackcloth from the greatest to the least of them" (v. 5).

Despite Jonah's lack of enthusiasm, the message spreads like wildfire through the city, the people believe and respond immediately. Everyone started fasting and dressing in sackcloth—universal signs of repentance.

Eventually, the news of coming judgement reaches the palace.

"When the word reached the king of Nineveh, he arose from his throne, laid aside his robe from him, covered himself with sackcloth and sat on the ashes. He issued a proclamation and it said, 'In Nineveh by the decree of the king and his nobles: Do not let man, beast, herd, or flock taste a thing. Do not let them eat or drink water. But both man and beast must be covered with sackcloth; and let men call on God earnestly that each may turn from his wicked way and from the violence which is in his hands. Who knows, God may turn and relent and withdraw His burning anger so that we will not perish'" (vv. 6–9).

Like his people, the king hears this prophecy of an unknown god given by an unknown prophet, but believes it, and responds immediately and dramatically. The whole city moves to mourning, turning from their violent ways, and throwing themselves on the possibility that this God may just extend mercy to them.

For the second time in the book of Jonah we find the attitudes and actions of pagans being depicted as godlier than those of God's prophet. Just as the sailors called out to God, tried to spare Jonah's life, and vowed and sacrificed to Yahweh, we also find the awful Ninevites responding immediately and dramatically to the word of God. In both cases, the pagans are used as foils against which Jonah is compared and shown to be lacking godliness.

The entire city, from the greatest to the least, the king to the beggar (and even the animals), repented of sin. Yet, to this point, God's prophet has done no such thing.

In chapter 3 of this book we find, yet again, a negative example in Jonah in that he lacks compassion for "the outsider."

What about God? What is *God's heart for "the outsider"*?

God's compassion was already on display in chapter 1 when he commissioned Jonah to warn Nineveh instead of destroying them and again in chapter 3 when he recommissioned Jonah. God's compassion was also seen in his dealings with Jonah.

And, finally, as we come to the last verse of chapter 3, we see his heart for "the outsider" on display yet again: "When God saw their deeds, that they turned from their wicked way, then God relented concerning the calamity which He had declared He would bring upon them. And He did not do it" (v. 10).

This verse describes the *opposite* of what Jonah desired and the *culmination* of what God desired.

Jonah's heart was that Nineveh would be punished for their evil; God's was that Nineveh would turn from that evil and experience mercy. Whereas Jonah's heart for "the outsider" was indifference, God's was love and compassion.

And praise God for this because, though we sometimes forget (just as Jonah seemed to have forgotten), we too were "outsiders" to whom God extended his love and compassion.

"But God demonstrates His own love toward us, in that while we were yet sinners, Christ died for us" (Rom 5:8).

It was while we were separated from God in rebellion and wickedness—outside his grace, outside a relationship with him, outside forgiveness, outside reconciliation, outside the family of God—that God came after us, sending not a fickle prophet like Jonah, but the perfect Prophet in his

Son, Jesus, who came to proclaim the ultimate message of love, mercy, and compassion. You see, every one of us, as believers, were once standing in the streets of Nineveh when we heard the liberating and powerful proclamation of the gospel. We were outsiders, and God showed us indescribable compassion.

And this is now when we have to look in the mirror of the Bible, ask ourselves honestly what's being reflected back at us, and ask the Holy Spirit to help us apply what we see rather than forget it. We want to be doers and not just hearers.

Is my heart for "the outsider"—those that don't look like me, talk like me, think like me; those that attend a different church, who are of a different religion, who are trapped in a creepy cult; those that may even be considered my ideological opponents; those I disagree with politically, spiritually, intellectually; those who are criminals, rebels, or dangerous; those who have hurt me in the past, embarrassed me, disappointed me, shunned me—is my heart for these "outsiders" like Jonah's or like God's?

Are there people, or groups of people, that, if I'm honest, I'm indifferent about when it comes to their eternal destiny or their current standing before a holy God. Maybe I'm even vengeful.

When I think of those "outsiders," and they can be different for each of us, but when I think of them, do I long to reflect to them God's compassion and mercy? Would I sincerely celebrate upon hearing they were shown compassion?

It's not always enjoyable looking in the mirror, is it? But it's healthy, especially when that mirror is Scripture, our guide is the Holy Spirit, and the goal is Christlikeness.

And Christlikeness, godliness, in this case demands we *Love across all lines! Love across all lines!* That God is progressively developing in each of us a growing desire to see God's compassion extend beyond any boundary there is, whether it's a real boundary or one we've made up. We're to *Love across all lines!*

I challenge you this week to think of a single person in your life that you would consider an "outsider" for whatever reason. Maybe they've hurt you in the past, maybe they're mean and rude and dismissive of your faith, maybe they're of another religion. Think of a single person, and before we meet again as a church, let's do three things.

First, remember that we were once outsiders. If not for God's initiative, his grace, his compassion, his mercy, we would be forever lost. Remember that we were once outsiders.

I've heard it said, "We [Christians] are never more than poor beggars telling other poor beggars where there is bread." Jonah forgot his outsider roots. We must not. We must remember that we were once outsiders.

Second, pray for that outsider, the one God brought to mind. I doubt Jonah could have prayed for Nineveh. To pray for someone is to love them. So, let's pray for that outsider, that they would experience God's compassion and love (even if it means, through us!).

Third, reach out to that outsider. A phone call, a text, a communication-starting email. Whatever it looks like, commit to making contact with hopes that it leads to an opportunity to reflect God's compassionate character to this individual.

Remember that we were outsiders. Pray for the outsider. Reach out to the outsider.

Brothers and sisters, let's be a people who, unlike Jonah and more like God, *Love across all lines!* Let's be, empowered by the Holy Spirit, committed to reflecting God's compassionate character to those around us, even those we struggle to believe deserve it, remembering that neither did we.

REFLECTING GOD'S COMPASSION
. . . SUBMISSIVELY (JONAH 4)

Sermon Map

Theological Focus
The people of God reflect the compassionate character of the God who has called them by understanding and submitting to his will at the expense of their own.

Introduction

[Image] A review leading to chapter 4 and the pouting prophet angry with God

[Need] The text puts before God's people a list of objectively good assignments from God: obey and enjoy (chapter 1), pray with God (chapter 2), and love across all lines (chapter 3)! Who doesn't want to do these things!?

[Topic] What stops God's people from "obeying and enjoying" God's blessings, from "praying with God" rather than against him, from loving "across all lines"? What stops God's people from reflecting God's compassionate character to those around us?

[Reference] As we now come to the culmination of the book of Jonah— chapter 4—we're going to find the answer to that question.

[Organization] What we're going to see from this chapter and, really, from the book as a whole, is that it's not an understanding problem, but a submission problem. That is to say, what stops us from doing what God has called us to do in this world (reflecting his compassionate character to those around us) has little to do with a lack of clarity of the assignment and more to do with a dogged unwillingness to sacrifice anything to do what we're told. It's not an understanding problem, it's a submission problem.

Body

[Entry signpost] And it's this closing interaction between God and prophet that reveals not only what has been Jonah's problem throughout, but also what may be our problem today.

I. It's not an understanding problem . . .

    A. God's revealed desire—a desire that is consistent with his character—must be understood if God's people are going to reflect his compassionate character to those around them.

        1. Jonah already understood God's character (vv. 1–2)
        NOTE: Second prayer; self-righteous as the first (ch. 2)

        2. God graciously illustrated his character for Jonah (vv. 6–11)

    B. Relevance: Like Jonah, it's difficult for us to say we don't understand God's character and his desire to show compassion to all people. He's made it known.

    [Illustration] Arrested for stealing though it's a known crime

[Transition] God's people are to reflect God's compassion to the world. When we fail to do that, it's not for lack of information. It's not an *understanding* problem that Jonah had and that we have.

II. . . . It's a submission problem

    A. God's revealed desire must not only be understood, but it must be submitted to if God's people are to reflect his compassionate character to those around them.

        1. What Jonah understood about God he called "evil" (vv. 1, 3–5; cp. v. 6)

        2. Jonah's desires conflicted with God's, and he didn't want to give them up (vv. 4–17).

        3. What happens when we fail to submit our desires to God's? (1) We're "evil." Jonah and Nineveh have traded places; while Nineveh was said to be evil (1:2; 3:2), now Jonah's lack of submission to God is evil (4:1). (2) We take God's place as judge.

    B. Relevance: And, like Jonah, sometimes you and I have submission problems. We don't want to give up what *we* desire for what we *know* God desires. The motives for this disobedience are myriad, but it always comes down to a simple unwillingness.

[Illustration] The culture's aversion to authority beyond the self

[Transition] Jonah didn't have an understanding problem, he had a submission problem. And you and I are brought into this story in verse 12. Look with me. Oh, wait, there is no verse 12.

III. *Love 'til it hurts!*

- Write a twelfth verse in your Bible: "Love 'til it hurts!"
- Go back to that person from last week; reach out again.

Sermon Manuscript

We come to the final chapter of the book of Jonah, a well-known and often-told biblical story that, as we've been discovering, has more to say than perhaps some of us realized.

The book is about more than an emotional prophet and a hungry whale. It's about God's compassionate character and how we, as God's people, are to reflect that divine compassion to the world around us like the moon reflects the sun, giving light to the darkest of nights. This assignment to be compassion reflectors is revealed primarily through the *negative* example of the title character—the prophet, Jonah—who fails to do what readers of the text, like you and I, are being called to do.

In the opening chapter we witnessed *a prodigal prophet running from God*. Jonah rebelled against God and found himself leaving, not God's presence like he wanted, but God's blessings. And, looking at Jonah's mistake, we felt the simple but profound call upon our lives to *Obey and enjoy!* We are called to *reflect God's compassion obediently* and then enjoy the blessings that certainly follow.

In chapter 2 we saw *a pious prophet praying against God*. As Jonah called to God from the fish belly he did so with impure motives and full of self-righteousness. And that reminds and motivates you and me to be a people that *Pray* with *God!* and not against him, that we are invited to *reflect God's compassion consistently*—that is, consistent with God's character.

In chapter 3 we found *a pedestrian prophet speaking for God*. Here God's heart for the outsider was on display as he showed compassion to a repentant Nineveh. In contrast, Jonah showed callousness and vindictiveness. We, wanting to be more like God than Jonah, were called to *Love across all lines!* and not be selective with our efforts but *reflect God's compassion indiscriminately*.

I suspect that very few Christians would find that list disagreeable. In fact, I think most would say we want to live a life that reflects God's compassion obediently, consistently, and indiscriminately. We want to be people who obey and enjoy, who pray with God, and who love across all lines. These are undeniably good things!

The question then becomes, what stops us from doing them? They sound great, they sound divine, they sound powerful. So, why is it a struggle to carry them out with regularity? Why do I still sometimes disobey? Why does self-righteousness continue to creep into my prayers from time to time? Why is it a battle for me to love the outsiders in my life?

The closing chapter of the book provides us an answer. Turn to Jonah 4 if you haven't already. What we're going to find in this chapter is that our problem is not one of *understanding* but one of *submission*. That is, what stops us from doing what God has called us to do in this world—reflecting his compassion to those around us—has little to do with a lack of information and more to do with a lack of willingness to sacrifice. It's not an understanding problem; it's a submission problem.

While we've seen a prodigal prophet running from God, a pious prophet praying against God, and a pedestrian prophet speaking for God, as we come to the final scene of the book, we find *a pouting prophet angry with God*.

And it's this closing interaction between God and prophet that reveals not only what has been Jonah's problem throughout, but also what may be our problem today.

What stopped Jonah from doing what God called him to do? Well, first we see that *it's not an understanding problem*. The reason for Jonah's rebellion wasn't a lack of information or clarity. That wasn't his issue.

"He prayed to the Lord and said, 'Please Lord, was not this what I said while I was still in my own country? Therefore in order to forestall this I fled to Tarshish, for I knew that You are a gracious and compassionate God, slow to anger and abundant in lovingkindness, and one who relents concerning calamity'" (v. 2).

After begrudgingly delivering God's warning message to evil Nineveh, Jonah watched as God "relented concerning the calamity which He had declared He would bring upon them." God showed mercy, a mercy that ticked off Jonah who now turns to God and says, "Listen up while I tell you why I've been so mad and why I'm still mad now."

And what's the reason he gives? The reason he's so angry *with* God is that he *knows* God. Like his statement to the sailors in chapter 1, this prayer in 4:2 is full of good theology. Jonah knows well the God he has run from, the God with whom he is unhappy, and the God to whom he now speaks. It's *because* he knows God and God's character, that he ran away in the first place, trying to delay what he knew God would probably do, that is, be who he is: "gracious and compassionate, slow to anger and abundant in lovingkindness, and one who relents concerning calamity."

Not only did Jonah *not* reflect God's compassionate character, he's angry with God for *having* a consistently compassionate character.

Jonah's problem was not an *understanding* problem. He *knew* God, he *knew* God's character, he *knew* God's assignment. He couldn't claim ignorance.

And neither can we. There may be a season when a Christian, being new to the faith, is learning about God like drinking from a fire-hydrant. But as months and years pass, claims of ignorance become less legitimate.

It's like someone who gets arrested for stealing insisting they didn't know theft was a crime. Either they're lying and *did* know, or they're telling the truth and *should've* known. Either way, they're guilty.

We serve a God who has revealed himself, his character, his will, his plan, and his purposes. Even those who ignore God's self-revelation, Paul writes in Romans 1, "are without excuse" because creation itself screams with clarity God's "eternal power and divine nature."

God's people are to reflect God's compassion to the world. When we fail to do that, it's not for lack of information. It's not an *understanding* problem that Jonah had and that we have. What we find as we keep reading is that, actually, *it's a submission problem.*

"But it greatly displeased Jonah and he became angry" (v. 1). Literally, the Hebrew reads "It was very evil to Jonah." Jonah looked at Nineveh's repentance and God's mercy and says: "*That's* wicked!"

Just as God declares in the New Testament that all "have fallen short" of God's standard, so here Jonah says God has fallen short of Jonah's standard. The prophet sees God's compassion on display and declares it unjust, "evil," and, because of that, probably sees his own anger as righteous indignation. As a prophet, Jonah's job was to *speak* God's words, but here he has the audacity to *condemn* God's actions. He has put God on trial and declared him guilty.

"Therefore now, O Lord, please take my life from me, for death is better to me than life" (v. 3). Jonah would rather give up his life than live in a world where *Ninevite* lives are spared. But just like on the ship, Jonah won't do it himself and asks God to kill him.

The Lord, rightly, questions this logic: "The Lord said, 'Do you have good reason to be angry?' Then Jonah went out from the city and sat east of it. There he made a shelter for himself and sat under it in the shade until he could see what would happen in the city" (vv. 4–5).

God's question isn't for God's sake (he knows the answer) but for Jonah's, that he might re-think his anger and submit his perceived moral high ground to God's. But Jonah's response is to camp outside the city, watch and hope the repentance won't last or that God will come to his senses, see that Jonah is right, and destroy Nineveh after all.

You see, Jonah didn't have an *understanding* problem, he had a *submission* problem. And that's a problem we sometimes share, don't we? When Christians struggle with leading the type of lives God calls us to live, it's usually not because we don't *understand* him or his will, it's that we don't like it. It clashes with what *we* desire, what *we* picture, with what's easy, with what feels good, and with what the world says is right. It's not an understanding problem, it's a submission problem.

And we come by it honestly because the culture in which we live has a violent aversion to any authority beyond the self. Every truth claim—whether from government, teachers, parents, or experts in any field of study—is put on trial by individual sensibilities, preferences, and experiences. It's only true if I want it to be, if it doesn't offend me, contradict me, inconvenience me. We're encouraged to pursue and find and celebrate *our* truth, whatever that is. Parents, who are God-given authorities in the home, are told to listen to their children and let *them* guide their parenting. Political leaders know nothing, governmental documents are re-read in light of modern ideological movements, and God, if he exists at all, is made in our image and our likeness (not the other way around) and he exists only to affirm and encourage, never to correct or judge.

Any and every truth claim, no matter how patently obvious, can be—and we're told *should* be—rejected, dismissed, mocked, and demonized if they run opposed to the new sheriff in town: the self. If I don't like any truth claim, I deny it, not because there's evidence against it, but because there is no authority greater than me.

This is what the author of Judges was referring to when he lamented that "In those days there was no king in Israel; everyone did what was right in his own eyes" (21:25). There was no authority but the self.

Likewise, back in Romans 1, Paul writes, speaking of sinful humanity: "For even though they knew God (not an understanding problem), they did not honor Him as God (it's a submission problem) or give thanks, but they became futile in their speculations, and their foolish heart was darkened. Professing to be wise, they became fools, and exchanged the glory of the incorruptible God for an image in the form of corruptible man (the self) . . ."

In the time of the Judges, in the time of Paul, and in our time today, it's the same thing. Humanity doesn't have an *understanding* problem; we have a *submission* problem. God has revealed himself and instead of submitting as unto the perfect Authority and definer of reality that he is, humanity turns away, thinking ourselves really wise, but in actuality proving ourselves unspeakably foolish.

And because this is the water in which we swim (because this anti-authoritarianism is all around us), even as God's people we must battle this submission problem. Jonah had to as well, didn't he?

Getting back to the actual text of Jonah we find that the book closes with God trying to solidify this lesson in the mind of his prophet through the use of an object lesson.

"So the Lord God appointed a plant and it grew up over Jonah to be a shade over his head to deliver him from his discomfort. And Jonah was extremely happy about the plant.

"But God appointed a worm when dawn came the next day and it attacked the plant and it withered. When the sun came up God appointed a scorching east wind, and the sun beat down on Jonah's head so that he became faint and begged with all his soul to die, saying, 'Death is better to me than life.'

"Then God said to Jonah, 'Do you have good reason to be angry about the plant?' And he said, 'I have good reason to be angry, even to death.'

"Then the Lord said, 'You had compassion on the plant for which you did not work and which you did not cause to grow, which came up overnight and perished overnight. Should I not have compassion on Nineveh, the great city in which there are more than 120,000 persons who do not know the difference between their right and left hand, as well as many animals'" (vv. 6–11)?

God exposed the root of the issue. Jonah cares more about his own comfort and agenda than about anything else in this world, including his relationship with the God he knows so well.

In verse 9, God gives Jonah one last chance to see his own foolishness: "Are you serious about this plant, Jonah?" To which Jonah responds: "As serious as a heart attack."

Then God drops the hammer: "Let me get this straight: You love this plant so much—which you had nothing to do with and which comes and goes—and I, God Almighty, am not allowed, in your estimation, to have compassion on the people of Nineveh, whom I made and love? They have eternal souls!"

You see, Jonah *knew* God. That wasn't his problem. His problem was he wasn't *submitting* to God. Instead, he wanted God to submit to *him*, to do things *his* way, think the way *he* thought, care about the things *he* cared about, and, especially in this case, hate the things *he* hated. The prophet had it backwards. Jonah didn't have an *understanding* problem; he had a *submission* problem.

The book of Jonah reminds us that God is a compassionate God who desires his people to reflect that compassion to the world. We are to do that *obediently, consistently, indiscriminately,* and now, in chapter 4, *submissively*—to default to God's authority. We are to submit to him, his will, his character, his demands, his description of reality, his word, his rebuke, his correction, his church. We, as God's people, are to reflect God's compassion *submissively*. He's God, we're not.

So, in the book of Jonah we've been called to obey and enjoy, to pray *with* God, and to love across all lines. As we come to the end of our study we're met with a final invitation: We're to *Love 'til it hurts!* Love 'til it hurts! We're to love God and others to the point where we are having to sacrifice our own preferences and sensibilities on the altar of obedience to God. Love to the point where we empty ourselves of any entitlement or claim on our own lives.

This may mean submitting to authorities God has put in place, relinquishing our precious autonomy. It may mean standing for a biblical truth around people who reject that reality and the authority of Scripture. It may mean obedience to God even when we don't like it, feel like we don't agree with it, or want to explain and justify away our rebellion. This is loving 'til it hurts!

Jesus clearly said "If anyone wishes to come after Me, he must deny himself, and take up his cross and follow Me. For whoever wishes to save his life will lose it; but whoever loses his life for My sake will find it" (Matt 16:24–25). That verse hurts! Self-denial hurts. Cross carrying hurts. Life abandonment hurts. But, according to Christ, and as we've seen negatively in Jonah, it's the way to true life. So, we love 'til it hurts, submitting all we are, all we think, all we plan to the One who has authority anyway.

This week, I suggest that you reread the last two verses of the book of Jonah every day and let its open-endedness haunt you and guide your prayers. Let's do that again right now:

"Then the Lord said, 'You had compassion on the plant for which you did not work and which you did not cause to grow, which came up overnight and perished overnight. Should I not have compassion on Nineveh, the great city in which there are more than 120,000 persons who do not know the difference between their right and left hand, as well as many animals'" (vv. 10–11).

We're left hanging for a reason, because God's question is not only directed to Jonah, but at you and me as well. Do we care for that which God cares for, submitting our emotions, dreams, preferences, sensibilities, and everything else to him, or do we, like his prophet, expect God to bend to ours? Do we put him on trial? Are there commands of God that, if I'm honest, make me blush? Are there things he's said that I don't agree with? Do we look at that which he commands and does and call it "evil"? Let these two Spirit-inspired verses search your heart this week and reveal anything Jonah-like that needs to be dealt with, confessed to God, and covered with God's forgiveness.

The book of Jonah is an invitation to the abundant life God wants us to live, a life of blessing, usefulness, significance, worth, power, love, grace, excitement, peace, reconciliation, and joy.

It's an invitation to an intimate relationship with the Creator and Sustainer of all things.

It's an invitation to impact the world in which we live in the only sustainable and significant way that there is—by reflecting God's character, by God's power, with God's message, and for God's glory.

Appendix C

Survey for the Book of Jonah

THE FOLLOWING PAGES INCLUDE the research instrument developed for the purpose of this study with the three hypotheses in mind. This survey was distributed, completed, and submitted prior to the start of the Jonah sermon series. Upon completion of the four-week series, the survey again was distributed, completed, and submitted for comparison.

UNDERSTANDING AND APPLYING
THE BOOK OF JONAH[1]

Thank you so much for your help in this project! The information you provide in this survey is critical to my research. In an effort to guard your anonymity and track your responses, please label this document in the space provided below following these guidelines:

        The second letter of your last name (surname)

+   The day of your birth (two numbers)

+   The first letter of the name of your home street

        ————————————

=   Your tracking code

Example #1:

        Amanda L**Y**NN

+   January **01**, 2001

+   900 **R**athburn Road W.

        ————————————

=   **Y01R**

Example #2:

        Stanley K**U**PP

+   March **17**, 1893

+   30 **Y**onge Street

        ————————————

=   **U17Y**

Your tracking code

——— ——— ——— ———

---

1. For a description *of* and rationale *for* the development of this tool, see "Research Method and Procedures: An Overview" and "Research Instrument" both in chapter 3.

Let's start with some questions about you.

Sex: ☐ Male ☐ Female

Age: ☐ < 12 ☐ 12–17☐ 18–24☐ 25–34☐ 35–44☐ 45–54☐ 55–64
        ☐ 65–74☐ 75+

How many years have you been a Christian?

        ☐ < 1   ☐ 1–4   ☐ 5–9   ☐ 10–14☐ 15–19☐ 20+

Do you have any formal Bible training?

☐ No   ☐ Camp
☐ Some Bible college   ☐ Bible college degree
☐ Some seminary   ☐ Seminary degree

How often do you attend a corporate, Sunday morning worship service at
    your church?

☐ 1–4 times per year   ☐ About once a month
☐ About every-other week   ☐ Basically every Sunday

When you do attend church, where do you go?

☐ Oakridge Bible Chapel   ☐ Other

Now to the main course!

Without consulting your Bible or any other resource, circle the best an-
swer to the following questions. *Don't be discouraged* if you find it tough!
Remember, you're going to get another shot at this after working through
Jonah as a church family.

1. In the first chapter of Jonah, God sent the prophet to _____ but he
    went to _____.

    (a) Tarshish, Nineveh   (b) Nineveh, Jerusalem
    (c) Nineveh, Tarshish   (d) Jerusalem, Tarshish
    (e) Jerusalem, Babylon   (f) Babylon, Jerusalem

2. What was Jonah's stated motivation for disobeying God in chapter 1?

    (a) Fleeing God's assignment   (b) Fleeing God's presence
    (c) Fleeing wickedness   (d) Fleeing God's judgement
    (e) The chapter doesn't tell us (f) I'm not sure

3. What was the result of Jonah's disobedience in chapter 1?
   (a) Loss of divine blessing   (b) Loss of prophetic position
   (c) Loss of salvation   (d) Loss of physical health
   (e) Both (b) and (d)   (f) All of the above

4. What best describes the main point, *thrust,*[2] or focus that God is communicating through the text of Jonah 1? (Note: While all below statements may be taught in the Bible, not all are the primary teaching of this particular chapter.)
   (a) No matter how hard the attempt and how far the retreat, God's people cannot escape God's presence and plan.
   (b) Jesus, in his obedience to the Father, is the "perfect Jonah," successfully accomplishing the task the disobedient prophet failed to accomplish.
   (c) God's people are to flee wickedness and judgement, not righteousness and opportunities for evangelism.
   (d) To run from opportunities to demonstrate God's compassion to others is to forfeit divine blessings.
   (e) The disobedience of God's people negatively affects not only them but often those around them.
   (f) Provide your own: _____
   _____

5. What best describes the *divine demand*[3] God places upon readers of Jonah 1? In other words, *from this passage of Scripture,* God's people are called to . . .
   (a) Obediently show godly compassion to others and enjoy the subsequent blessings.
   (b) Identify how God angers and disappoints us and confess that arrogance to Him.
   (c) Run *toward* God, understanding the futility of fleeing *from* Him.
   (d) Run *from* (wickedness) and *toward* (righteousness) that which God prescribes.
   (e) Obediently take opportunities to share the gospel with others.
   (f) Provide your own: _____
   _____

2. The *thrust* of a text refers to what the Author is *doing* with what he is *saying.* He is using words to accomplish something, and the *thrust* is an attempt to succinctly articulate what that is!

3. The *divine demand* is the specific call of God in a specific passage of Scripture for his people to live a specific way for their good and his glory.

6. Understanding the *thrust* and *divine demand* of Jonah 1, what is the most appropriate *applicational command*[4] for God's people today?

   (a) Obey and enjoy!   (b) Run *to* not *from* God!
   (c) Share the gospel!   (d) Be like Jesus *not* Jonah!
   (e) Submit to God's plan!   (f) Other: _____

7. What is the setting of the second chapter of Jonah?

   (a) A ship deck   (b) A fish stomach
   (c) A foreign city   (d) The text doesn't say
   (e) Jerusalem   (f) I don't know

8. What is the *main* literary genre of Jonah 2?

   (a) Psalm / poetry   (b) Narrative / story
   (c) Prophetic   (d) A combination of genres
   (e) A genre unique to Jonah   (f) I'm not sure

9. What is the emotional tenor of Jonah 2? In other words, according to the text, what is the best description of the prophet's mood and/or heart condition at this point of the story?

   (a) Self-righteous, hypocritical   (b) Fearful, rebuked, humbled
   (c) Thankful, repentant   (d) Reverent, worshipful
   (e) Both (c) and (d)   (f) I'm not sure

10. What best describes the main point, *thrust*, or focus that God is communicating through the text of Jonah 2? (Note: While all below statements may be taught in the Bible, not all are the primary teaching of this particular chapter.)

   (a) Like Jesus in the Garden of Gethsemane, God's people are to call out to Him in times of suffering, oppression, and grief.
   (b) The prayers of God's people should reflect a heart that is consistent with the character of the God to whom they pray.
   (c) Regardless of the depths of disobedience to which God's people may fall, God's grace is sufficient to deliver, redeem, and reconcile.
   (d) The tasks to which God calls his people are always for *our* good and for *his* glory, regardless of how they may seem.
   (e) For his people, thanksgiving is the only appropriate response to God's gracious deliverance from the consequences of our sin.
   (f) Provide your own: _____

4. Rooted in a right understanding of a passage's *thrust* and *divine demand*, an *applicational command* is an authoritative assignment from God to his people.

11. What best describes the *divine demand* God places upon readers of Jonah 2? In other words, *from this passage of Scripture*, God's people are called to . . .

    (a) Trust that God's will is *always* good and right and, as such, should be followed even without total understanding.

    (b) Live lives marked by thankfulness for all God *has* done, *is* doing, and *will* do both for us and for the whole world.

    (c) Even in times of crises, ask ourselves "what would Jesus (not Jonah) do?"

    (d) Pray prayers that are consistent with the compassionate character of God.

    (e) Call out to God for deliverance no matter the depth of our current sin.

    (f) Provide your own: _____

    _____

12. Understanding the *thrust* and *divine demand* of Jonah 2, what is the most appropriate *applicational command* for God's people today?

    (a) Trust God always!   (b) Live *thankful* lives!

    (c) Pray *with* God!   (d) When in *deep*, call to be lifted *up*!

    (e) Praise God always!   (f) Other: _____

13. What happens to the prophet that marks the *beginning* of Jonah 3?

    (a) Rebuked by God   (b) Thrown into the sea

    (c) Swallowed   (d) Forgiven by God

    (e) Recommissioned by God   (f) I'm not sure

14. Regardless of how it begins, chapter 3 finds Jonah serving as God's mouthpiece to a specific people. What is the main tone of the message he is given to proclaim?

    (a) Believe the gospel!   (b) Judgement is coming!

    (c) God loves you!   (d) Leave Israel alone!

    (e) Both (b) and (c)   (f) I'm not sure

15. The people to whom Jonah preaches respond to his message with _____ and thus, God responds with _____.

    (a) Repentance, eternal life   (b) Fear, judgement

    (c) Fear, compassion   (d) Repentance, mercy

    (e) Unbelief, judgement   (f) Belief, forgiveness

16. What best describes the main point, *thrust*, or focus that God is communicating through the text of Jonah 3? (Note: While all below statements may be taught in the Bible, not all are the primary teaching of this particular chapter.)

   (a) The God of the Bible is the God of second chances, always being willing to use his people if they will walk in obedience and submission to his revealed will.
   (b) God, being gracious and loving, desires his message of reconciliation to spread to *all* nations, a desire that found its full realization in the gospel of Jesus Christ.
   (c) Forgiveness, reconciliation, and mercy are *always* available to *all* who will humble themselves in repentance toward God and his word.
   (d) The gospel, a message powerful enough to change lives eternally, is surprisingly simple and understandable.
   (e) God's people are to indiscriminately reflect and demonstrate God's compassionate character to others, regardless of their perceived worthiness.
   (f) Provide your own: _____

17. What best describes the *divine demand* God places upon readers of Jonah 3? In other words, *from this passage of Scripture*, God's people are called to . . .

   (a) Reflect God's desire to demonstrate his compassionate character to all people, regardless of their perceived worthiness of such grace.
   (b) Remember the KISS principle: Keep It (the gospel message) Simply, Silly!
   (c) Continue Jonah's assignment, taking the news of God's offer of forgiveness and reconciliation to all people.
   (d) Live lives marked by humble repentance and obedience toward God.
   (e) Thank God for the patience and graciousness he often shows us in spite of our disobedience.
   (f) Provide your own: _____

18. Understanding the *thrust* and *divine demand* of Jonah 3, what is the most appropriate *applicational command* for God's people today?

   (a) Obey the *first* time!   (b) Repent and live well!
   (c) Spread the news!   (d) Thank God for second chances!
   (e) Love across all lines (like God)! (f) Other: _____

19. Who are the characters explicitly involved in Jonah 4?

   (a) God, Jonah   (b) God, Jonah, the sailors
   (c) God, Jonah, Israel   (d) God, Jonah, Foreigners
   (e) God, Jonah, the angel   (f) I'm not sure

20. In Jonah 4, the posture of the prophet's heart could be described as
_____ while God responds with _____.

   (a) Unrepentant, compassion   (b) Worshipful, correction
   (c) Humble, love   (d) Contrite, forgiveness
   (e) Calloused, judgement   (f) Thankful, mercy

21. In speaking with Jonah in chapter 4, which of the following does God
use to illustrate the lesson he desires the prophet (and us!) to learn?

   (a) A little worm   (b) A booming voice
   (c) A big fish   (d) A hot wind
   (e) Both (a) and (b)   (f) Both (a) and (d)

22. What best describes the main point, *thrust*, or focus that God is communicating through the text of Jonah 4? (Note: While all the below
statements may be biblical, not all are the primary teaching of this
particular chapter of Scripture.)

   (a) As an extension of his character, God shows mercy to whom he will
       show mercy, offering salvation to even the most vile sinner.
   (b) God's people are to reflect God's compassion to others by under-
       standing and submitting to his will at the expense of their own.
   (c) For God's people, anger and frustration with God and his ways re-
       veals the idolatry, prejudice, and sinfulness in our hearts.
   (d) Like Jesus, God's people are to confront prejudices in our world;
       unlike Jesus, sometimes they exist within our own hearts.
   (e) God's sovereignty in salvation (that he wisely and powerfully decides
       to whom he will extend compassion and mercy) is true regardless of
       how his people understand and accept that reality.
   (f) Provide your own: _____
       _____

23. What best describes the *divine demand* God places upon readers of
Jonah 4? In other words, *from this passage of Scripture*, God's people
are called to . . .

   (a) Stand against all forms of oppression and prejudices in this world.
   (b) Trust that God is *totally* sovereign and *perfectly* good in his work of
       salvation.
   (c) Praise God for the compassion, mercy, and power he puts on display
       in the salvation of each and every repentant sinner.
   (d) Be compassionate as God is compassionate, sacrificing their own
       agendas and desires in the process if necessary.
   (e) Avoid anger, disappointment, and frustration with God by growing
       in their knowledge of his perfect character.
   (f) Provide your own: _____

24. Understanding the *thrust* and *divine demand* of Jonah 4, what is the most appropriate *applicational command* for God's people today?

    (a) Trust God's sovereignty!   (b) Know God better!

    (c) Love sacrificially!   (d) Repent and believe!

    (e) Praise the God who saves!   (f) Other: _____

25. Considering the book of Jonah *in its entirety*, what would you consider the main theme the text itself highlights?

    (a) God's compassion   (b) God's sovereignty

    (c) God's patience   (d) Human dis/obedience

    (e) Reconciliation   (f) Other: _____

Thank you for your help!

Please return the completed survey in one of the following ways:

- Slide it under the [pastor's] office door
- Slide it under the [main church] office door
- Place it in the [pastor's] family church mailbox
- Place it in the church mailbox

Bibliography

Adams, Jay E. *Preaching with Purpose: The Urgent Task of Homiletics.* Grand Rapids: Zondervan, 1982.

Allen, David L. "Expository Preaching and the Mission of the Church." *Journal for Baptist Theology & Ministry* 6 (2009) 25–32.

Allen, Jason K. *Letters to My Students.* Vol. 1: *On Preaching.* Nashville: Broadman & Holman, 2019.

Ash, Christopher. *The Priority of Preaching.* Fearn, Scotland: Christian Focus, 2010.

Bailey, Mark. *To Follow Him: The Seven Marks of a Disciple.* Sisters: Multnomah, 1997.

Banting, Blayne A. *Take Up and Preach: A Primer for Interpreting Preaching Texts.* Eugene, OR: Wipf & Stock, 2016.

Beeke, Joel R. *Reformed Preaching: Proclaiming God's Word from the Heart of the Preacher to the Heart of His People.* Wheaton, IL: Crossway, 2018.

Beeke, Joel R., and Dustin W. Benge, eds. *Pulpit Aflame: Essays in Honor of Steven J. Lawson.* Grand Rapids: Reformation Heritage, 2016.

Begg, Alistair. *Preaching for God's Glory.* Wheaton, IL: Crossway, 1999

Birley, Graham, and Neil Moreland. *A Practical Guide to Academic Research.* London: Kogan Page, 1998.

Blomberg, Craig. *Matthew.* New American Commentary. Nashville: Broadman & Holman, 1992.

Blythe, Stuart. "The Place of Preaching in the Church's Mission Luke 4:16–30." *Journal of the Evangelical Homiletics Society* 19 (2019) 46–67.

Breneman, Mervin. *Ezra, Nehemiah, Esther.* New American Commentary. Nashville: Broadman & Holman, 1993.

Calvin, John. *Institutes of the Christian Religion.* Translated by Henry Beveridge. Peabody, MA: Hendrickson, 2008.

Chapell, Bryan. *Christ-Centered Preaching: Redeeming the Expository Sermon.* 2nd ed. Grand Rapids: Baker, 2005.

Chou, Abner. "A Hermeneutical Evaluation of the Christocentric Hermeneutic." *The Master's Seminary Journal* 27 (2016) 113–39.

Cone, Christopher. *Integrating Exegesis and Exposition: Biblical Communication for Transformative Learning.* Fort Worth, TX: Exegetica, 2015.

Dever, Mark. *Nine Marks of a Healthy Church.* Wheaton, IL: Crossway, 2004.

Dever, Mark, and Greg Gilbert. *Preach: Theology Meets Practice.* Nashville: Broadman & Holman, 2012.

Fowler, Floyd J., Jr. *Survey Research Methods.* 3rd ed. Thousand Oaks, CA: Sage, 2002.

Frost, Jim. "One-Tailed and Two-Tailed Hypothesis Tests Explained." Statistics by Jim. https://statisticsbyjim.com/hypothesis-testing/one-tailed-two-tailed-hypothesis-tests/.

Gibson, Scott M., ed. *The Worlds of the Preacher: Navigating Biblical, Cultural, and Personal Contexts*. Grand Rapids: Baker Academic, 2018.

Gibson, Scott M., and Matthew D. Kim, eds. *Homiletics and Hermeneutics: Four Views on Preaching Today*. Grand Rapids: Baker Academic, 2018.

Gordon, T. David. *Why Johnny Can't Preach: The Media Have Shaped the Messengers*. Phillipsburg, NJ: P&R, 2009.

Greidanus, Sidney. *The Modern Preacher and the Ancient Text: Interpreting and Preaching Biblical Literature*. Grand Rapids: Eerdmans, 1988.

Griffiths, Jonathan I. *Preaching in the New Testament: An Exegetical and Biblical-Theological Study*. Downers Grove, IL: InterVarsity, 2017.

Guthrie, Donald. *The Pastoral Epistles: An Introduction and Commentary*. Tyndale New Testament Commentary. Downers Grove, IL: IVP Academic, 2015.

Hargrove, Carl A. "Implication and Application in Exposition: A Complementary Relationship, Part 1: Expositional Definitions and Applicational Categories." *The Master's Seminary Journal* 30 (2019) 65–91.

Hughes, R. Kent. *Disciplines of a Godly Man*. Wheaton, IL: Crossway, 2001.

Johnson, Darrell W. *The Glory of Preaching: Participating in God's Transformation of the World*. Downers Grove, IL: IVP Academic, 2009.

Jorgenson, Rodger L. "The Necessity of Contemporary Preaching." *The Covenant Quarterly* 30 (1972) 18–30.

Keller, Timothy. *Preaching: Communicating Faith in an Age of Skepticism*. New York: Penguin, 2016.

Kreider, Glenn R. *God with Us: Exploring God's Personal Interactions with His People throughout the Bible*. Phillipsburg, NJ: P&R, 2014.

Kuruvilla, Abraham. *1–2 Timothy, Titus: A Theological Commentary for Preachers*. Eugene, OR: Cascade, 2021.

———. "Christiconic Interpretation." *Bibliotheca Sacra* 173 (2016) 131–46.

———. *Ephesians: A Theological Commentary for Preachers*. Eugene, OR: Cascade, 2015.

———. *Genesis: A Theological Commentary for Preachers*. Eugene, OR: Resource, 2014.

———. *Judges: A Theological Commentary for Preachers*. Eugene, OR: Cascade, 2017.

———. *A Manual for Preaching: The Journey from Text to Sermon*. Grand Rapids: Baker Academic, 2019.

———. *Mark: A Theological Commentary for Preachers*. Eugene, OR: Cascade, 2012.

———. "Pericopal Theology." *Bibliotheca Sacra* 173 (2016) 3–17.

———. *Privilege the Text!: A Theological Hermeneutic for Preaching*. Chicago: Moody, 2013.

———. *A Vision for Preaching: Understanding the Heart of Pastoral Ministry*. Grand Rapids: Baker Academic, 2015.

Lamb, Jonathan. *Preaching Matters: Encountering the Living God*. Leicester: InterVarsity, 2014.

Lawson, Steven J. *The Heroic Boldness of Martin Luther*. Sanford, FL: Reformation Trust, 2013.

———. *The Kind of Preaching God Blesses*. Eugene, OR: Harvest House, 2013.

Lloyd-Jones, D. Martyn. *Preaching & Preachers*. Grand Rapids: Zondervan, 2012.

Long, Thomas G. "The Use of Scripture in Contemporary Preaching." *Interpretation* 44 (1990) 341–52.

Longman, Tremper, III, and David E. Garland, eds. *1 Chronicles–Job*. Expositor's Bible Commentary. Grand Rapids: Zondervan, 2010.

MacArthur, John. *Ashamed of the Gospel: When the Church Becomes Like the World*. Wheaton, IL: Crossway, 2010.

—. *Preaching: How to Preach Biblically*. Nashville: T. Nelson, 2005.

Maier, Walter A., III. "'Preach the Word' in the Old Testament." *Concordia Theological Quarterly* 66 (2002) 3–16.

Marshall, I. Howard. *Beyond the Bible: Moving from Scripture to Theology*. Grand Rapids: Baker Academic, 2004.

Mohler, R. Albert, Jr. *He Is Not Silent: Preaching in a Postmodern World*. Chicago: Moody, 2008.

Olford, Stephen F., and David L. Olford. *Anointed Expository Preaching*. Nashville: B&H Academic, 1998.

Pascal, Blaise. *Pensées and Other Writings*. Translated by Honor Levi. Edited by Anthony Levi. Oxford: Oxford University, 2008.

Porter, Stanley E., and Beth M. Stovell, eds. *Biblical Hermeneutics: Five Views*. Downers Grove, IL: InterVarsity, 2012.

Richard, Ramesh. *Preparing Expository Sermons: A Seven-Step Method for Biblical Preaching*. Grand Rapids: Baker, 2001.

Richardson, Kurt A. *James*. New American Commentary. Nashville: Broadman & Holman, 1997.

Robinson, Haddon W. *Biblical Preaching: The Development and Delivery of Expository Messages*. Grand Rapids: Baker, 1980.

—. "What Is Expository Preaching?" *Bibliotheca Sacra* 131 (1974) 55–60.

Spence-Jones, H. D. M., ed. *Ezra, Nehemiah, Esther, Job*. The Pulpit Commentary. New York: Funk & Wagnalls, 1909.

Stott, John R. W. *Between Two Worlds: The Art of Preaching in the Twentieth Century*. Grand Rapids: Eerdmans, 1982.

—. *I Believe in Preaching*. London: Hodder & Stoughton, 1982.

Sunukjian, Donald R. *Invitation to Biblical Preaching: Proclaiming Truth with Clarity and Relevance*. Grand Rapids: Kregel, 2007.

Swindoll, Charles R. *Saying It Well: Touching Others with Your Words*. New York: FaithWords, 2012.

Walvoord, John F., and Roy B. Zuck, eds. *The Bible Knowledge Commentary: New Testament*. Colorado Springs: Victor, 2000.

Willimon, Will. "Preaching: Acting Up with the Holy Spirit." *Journal for Preachers* 39 (2016) 2–6.

Yong, Amos. "Proclamation in/of the Spirit: Toward a Pneumatological Theology of Preaching." *The Living Pulpit* 24 (2015) 34–38.

York, Hershael W., and Scott A. Blue. "Is Application Necessary in the Expository Sermon?" *Southern Baptist Journal of Theology* 3 (1999) 70–73.

www.ingramcontent.com/pod-product-compliance
Lightning Source LLC
Chambersburg PA
CBHW060344100426
42812CB00003B/1116